50 plus one

Questions When Buying a Car

by
Stephen Edwards

Information to Encourage Achievement

1261 West Glenlake
Chicago, IL 60660
www.encouragementpress.com

ISBN: 1-933766-05-0

EAN: 978-1-933766-05-8

This product is not intended to provide legal or financial advice or substitute for the advice of an attorney or advisor.

10 9 8 7 6 5 4 3 2 1

©2007 Encouragement Press, LLC
1261 W. Glenlake
Chicago, IL 60660

Special discounts on bulk quantities of Encouragement Press books and products are available to corporations, professional associations and other organizations. For details, contact our Special Sales Department at 1.253.303.0033.

Questions When Buying a Car

About the Author

For more than 20 years, Stephen Edwards has been a regular contributor on a variety of consumer and business subjects, including books and articles about freelancing, starting a new business and marketing your company. In addition to Encouragement Press, Mr. Edwards has worked with publishers such as Probus Publishing, Times Mirror, McGraw Hill, Dartnell, Thompson International, Socrates Media and Scott Foresman and associations such as the American Medical Association, American Hospital Association and American Association of Neurological Surgeons.

Along with the title of accomplished author, Mr. Edwards is also an avid classic car buyer.

Acknowledgements

Special thanks . . . and cheers to the following:

Heather Hutchins, Maris Fineberg and Vernis Lewis

Table of Contents

Introduction

To paraphrase the famous quote, there are three things in life you cannot escape: death, taxes and the feeling that you just got hosed on the car you purchased or leased. For most people, buying a car will be the second most expensive purchase (repeated many times in life) you will make. Not only do you want the right car, but you want to have some assurance that you got the best deal, that you made the right decision on how to acquire the car and that, in general, you were a smart, savvy consumer.

As everyone clearly knows, car prices and fuel costs continue to rise–in many cases far beyond what can be thought to be reasonable. On the other hand, there is compelling evidence that cars are built better, last longer and are more efficient than ever before. There are also literally hundreds of choices in new, used and leased cars so that the average consumer–you–walk into the show room totally unprepared for the sheer number of issues to face and the decisions you need to make.

50 plue one Questions When Buying a Car is written with the consumer in mind. What is the best financing? Should you buy new or used? Is leasing a car a good idea? Which cars hold their value the longest? Should you have a used car inspected? Should you buy a car after the lease has expired?

These are just the beginning. There are literally hundreds of issues to learn about and make decisions on. Where you buy or lease a car is almost as important as the car you buy. Is buying from a dealer better than trying to buy a car directly from an individual? Are car auctions a good place to buy? How about the mega-centers which are so heavily advertised on television? Are they the best source for new and used cars?

When you have made your decision, how comfortable do you feel when you go into the deal room to haggle and negotiate with the manager? For most people, this is the most difficult part of the entire process–and often the most unpleasant.

This book can help you be prepared, ready to stand up and get the best deal possible.

A very important consideration is what you do with your old car: sell it, give it away to a friend or relative, trade it in or perhaps make a donation to one of the many charities asking for car and boat donations. You will find the answers, or least some good advice, on this and a dozen more topics.

Happy shopping! If you follow the advice in this book, you can save hundreds— even thousands of dollars on your next car.

Stephen Edwards

Is a Hybrid Car Right for Me?

The latest buzz from both the automakers and the media concerns hybrid cars (also called hybrid-electric cars or HEVs). Hybrids are cars with both an internal combustion engine that uses gasoline and an electric motor that uses rechargable batteries. Together this combination of green electricity and fossil fuel is supposed to offer better gas mileage while also helping to limit pollution, greenhouse gases and dependence on foreign oil.

While the hybrid models of the 1970s had to be plugged in every night, today's hybrids run exactly the same way that regular cars do. They are quite popular in many parts of the country.

The Challenge

Is a hybrid car right for you? That depends.

The proponents of hybrid cars point to their excellent gas efficiency and green motors. The mileage reported on many Websites lists in-town mileage of approximately 40 miles per gallon and highway mileage of up to 68 miles per gallon. These numbers look good considering the price of gasoline.

In addition, these vehicles are usually configured to run the gasoline engine for highway miles and the electric engine for start-and-stop city driving. For this reason, those who like hybrids claim that they will reduce pollution problems in cities while using less fossil fuel than conventional cars.

A major problem with hybrid cars is their bigger price tags–as much as $5,000 more than gasoline-engine cars. Some figures show that hybrid owners may not break even on their purchase until they have owned the car for 5 or more years.

Those who say that the hybrids are all hype also point to the Environmental Protection Agency's (EPA) recent comments that their mileage numbers for hybrid cars are at least 20 percent off. However, it seems that the EPA is using decades-old formulas to test hybrids and regular cars. The agency plans to retest cars next year once they have recalibrated their equipment and formulas.

If you are in favor of lower-emissions, less fossil fuel and a green way of life, you need to give hybrid cars a careful review. There are even green SUV models. They cost more, but are certainly greener than regular gasoline-powered vehicles. Another consideration that you need to keep in mind is that most hybrids have a long waiting list and it may take many months before you receive your vehicle.

The Facts

Emissions for Hybrid Cars

No doubt about it, hybrid cars have fewer emissions as regulated by the EPA. The big question is, fewer than what? Some Hondas and Toyotas are already pretty low on the emissions scale. You can compare the gas mileage and emissions on two hybrid cars or a hybrid and a regular car at the U.S. Department of Energy's Website at *www.energy.gov*.

Mileage for Hybrid Cars

According to the experts, hybrid cars get excellent gas mileage because they have two different motors. In most cases, the cars use the gasoline-powered engine on the highway and the battery-powered engine in the city. Despite the EPA's error range of 10 percent to 30 percent, the mileage numbers for hybrid cars are at least comparable to gasoline-only cars.

HEVs get from 40 to 70 miles per gallon according to the Department of Energy. As with conventional cars, the gas mileage is higher on the highway and less in the city. At the high end of the scale, the new Honda Insight is rated at 68 miles per gallon on the highway 61 miles per gallon in the city. The best-selling hybrid on the market, the Toyota Prius, is rated at 60 miles per gallon on the highway and 51 miles per gallon in the city. On the lower end of the scale, the Lexus GS 450h gets 28 miles per gallon on the highway and 25 miles per gallon in the city.

Safety for Hybrid Cars

Hybrid cars are as safe as the conventional cars on the road. The only different safety consideration is the electric motor and the batteries. Since, all hybrids have an automatic shut-off of both motors if the car is in an accident, hybrids are considered safe.

Types of Hybrid Cars

So far, Toyota (Prius, Camry, Highlander), Honda (Insight, Civic, Accord), Ford (Escape), Mercury (Mariner), and Lexus (RX 400h and GS 450h) have hybrid models for sale while other manufacturers have hybrid models coming out within the next year or so. Hybrids come in compact cars as you might expect, but they are also available in luxury cars and SUVs.

Although hybrids seem to be the most-hyped cars of the year, they account for only a little over 1 percent of the 17 million new cars sold each year in this country.

Speed and Pick-up of Hybrid Cars

Another myth about hybrids is that they are slow because they have smaller engines and better fuel efficiency. Drivers of these cars disagree. Since these cars have two motors, drivers and testers note that the pick-up and speed are the same as conventional cars. The only caveat is that for the best gas mileage, testers recommend that drivers limit their jackrabbit starts and tailgating. Most hybrid car Websites include a long list of driving tips to save gas and improve mileage.

Prices for Hybrid Cars

Hybrid cars cost more to produce and so they cost more to buy. Hybrids generally cost an average of $3,000 more per car than conventional automobiles. In some cases tax credits and increased gas mileage will cover the price tag over the life of the vehicle.

The Solutions

Proponents of hybrid cars point to all their advantages as selling points, but note that no one single item—such as gas mileage—should be the deciding factor. As they point out on various hybrid car Websites, car manufacturers and consumer groups have known for decades that the EPA's mileage numbers were off. This is not a surprise to anyone who has ever bought a new car and wondered why his or her mileage numbers never agreed with those published by the EPA.

Tax Credits

The federal government offers a tax credit for buying a hybrid car. The rate for 2005/2006 is $2,000. Additionally, many states have their own tax credits or rebates for buying a hybrid car. It is important to note that the fine print for the Internal Revenue Service (IRS) tax credit involves the number of hybrid cars that each manufacturer produces. When a manufacturer produces 60,000 cars, the tax credit is supposed to be phased out.

For the specifics of the tax credit and tax forms, go to *www.irs.gov*. Download the PDF versions of the Hybrid Electric Vehicle fact sheet and IRS *Publication 535*.

Saving the Planet by Depending Less on Fossil Fuels

Environmental Attorney Robert Kennedy was quoted on the hybridcars.com Website as saying our country could eliminate our gulf oil imports, "If we raised the fuel efficiency of American cars by 7.6 miles per gallon. If we raised it to only 2.7 miles per gallon, we would save enough oil to eliminate all the oil imports from Iraq and Kuwait combined."

This is a sobering thought, and the reason that many people choose to buy a hybrid car. Some people think that buying a gas-guzzling vehicle in these times is tantamount to supporting foreign countries that are often anti-American. While not everyone shares that view, most people agree that importing less foreign oil is a good way to help the economy and improve the environment at the same time.

Saving Money at the Gas Pump

Another reason to consider a hybrid car is your potential savings at the gas pump. However, if this is the only reason you would consider a hybrid car, then you might be better off with the newest compact cars that have greater fuel efficiency with a smaller price tag than their hybrid cousins.

Ultimately, the final decision to buy a hybrid vehicle is up to the individual. Even if the mileage figures from the EPA are off, hybrid cars do use less gasoline and pump out fewer pollutants into the environment.

The Resources

The following Websites offer more information about hybrid cars:

www.fueleconomy.gov

> This Website from the Department of Energy (DOE) includes information about all of the hybrid cars currently on the market.

www.safercar.gov

> National Highway Traffic Safety Administration's Website offers many helpful FAQs about hybrid cars.

www.hybridcars.com

> This is the Website for everything you ever wanted to know about hybrid cars.

www.msnbc.msn.com/id/12958916/site/newsweek

> Automotive writer, Keith Naughton, wrote an investigative piece for *Newsweek* magazine about hybrid cars that should be read if you are interested in hybrid cars.

1

Is It Time to Buy
a New Car?

These days most people are in either one camp or the other. According to CNW Marketing Research, four out of five people buy a new car before they actually need one. They buy because they want a shiny new car in the garage. That is Camp A.

Camp B includes those who keep their cars longer than their parents did. According to current statistics, the average car in the United States is 9 years old. That is the longest we have been keeping our cars since the 1950s when Eisenhower was president.

No matter which category best describes your inclinations, it can be tricky figuring out when to get a new (or new to you) car. You do not want to spend money unnecessarily, but you also do not want to wait until your old car falls apart on the highway before you find another.

The Challenge

There are no hard and fast rules about when to buy your next car. Each situation is different. However, you need to consider several factors before deciding what is best for you. These factors include the following:

- Financial
- Reliability
- Safety
- Fuel efficiency
- Lifestyle intangibles

The Facts

New Car Safety Devices

One reason to think about buying a newer car is safety. New cars have more standard safety features than ever before. Experts advise consumers to choose options that include extra air bags and other safety devices that can improve collision avoidance and injury.

Safety Devices on New Cars		
Type	**Name**	**Definition**
Active	Anti-lock brakes (ABS)	ABS usually prevents skids because the technology keeps the brakes from locking up.
	Brake assist	Studies have shown that drivers often hesitate before hitting the brakes in an emergency. Brake assist stops the car more quickly than the driver alone.
	Daytime running lights (DRL)	This new feature turns on the car's headlights automatically when the car is being driven.
	Electronic brake-force distribution (EBD)	This system distributes the braking pressure between the front and rear brakes, taking into account the speed of the car and conditions on the road.
	Tire pressure monitoring system (TPMS)	This feature should be available on all cars by 2007. The system monitors the pressure of all four tires and alerts the driver when one or more tires are underinflated.
	Traction control	This system helps you maintain control while speeding up, so you will be less likely to spin the tires in loose gravel or on a wet road.
	Vehicle stability control (VSC). Also called electronic stability control (ESC) or electronic stability system (ESS).	This system controls the ABS, traction controls and the way your vehicle moves from side to side to keep the car on the road.
	Vehicle dynamics integrated management (VDIM)	This system monitors the ABS, stability controls, road conditions, brakes and the other systems of the car to sense trouble before the driver is even aware of it.
Passive	• Front air bags • Side air bags • Side curtain air bags • Rollover air bags	New cars now have side air bags, curtain air bags and rollover air bags that protect you in a rollover accident, in addition to the front air bags that were only added a few years ago.
	Air bag disable switch	This feature is necessary for some people who might be hurt more by the air bag being deployed than by hitting the steering wheel or dashboard.
	Advanced safety belts	Seat belts include both a lap belt and a shoulder belt.
Kid Safety	Child safety seat tethers (LATCH)	This feature called LATCH (lower anchors and tethers for children) helps parents install their child's safety seat correctly. The straps anchor the child safety seat to the rear seat.

	Integrated child booster seats	Some new minivans include an option to add a child booster seat in the middle of the back seat.
Helpful Technology	Back-up sensing system	It is hard to run over people, animals or inanimate objects accidentally with this new feature. The car beeps at you when your vehicle backs up too close to an object.
	Night vision display	The night vision display projects the vehicle controls onto the inside of the windshield.

The Solutions

Five Key Issues

The final decision will be different for every family. You need to think about the five key issues mentioned above and analyzed below. Once you consider how you feel about all five points, you will know whether or not you need to buy a new car.

Financial considerations

Most consumers cite financial considerations as the primary reason they hesitate about buying a new car. New cars today cost in the range of $20,000 to $25,000 without adding in the extra expenses of taxes, fees and insurance.

If your old car is running well, you may decide to keep it because it is paid in full. However, if your old car is beginning to spend more time in the repair shop than in your garage, you may want to consider a newer vehicle. In general, experts advise that if your old car requires repairs that go well beyond the car's retail value, you should buy a newer car. If the repairs roughly equal the amount of a down payment on a new car (approximately $2,000), you should repair your old car.

Reliability

Reliability is another important factor. An older car is more likely to break down than a new car. In addition to the expense of repairing the car, there is also the issue of personal safety and timeliness to consider. What do you do if your car breaks down in the middle of nowhere? Will it be worth it to you if your car breaks down on the way to an important job interview or business meeting? If your old car is making you miss meetings or get to work late, you may want to consider buying a newer vehicle. You also need to consider the time that you will have to spend taking it to the repair shop, waiting for the estimate, then waiting until the car is fixed.

Safety

A third issue to consider is safety. New cars have advanced safety features such as the ones listed in the chart above. If you have a family, you will be interested in the door locks that children cannot open from inside the car. Newer cars also have air bags, stabilization and control systems that automatically adjust for weather and road conditions, in addition to computerized communications systems such as GM's On-Star™ program. If you are stranded anywhere in the United States, these communications systems can use GPS to locate you, give you directions or get help.

Fuel efficiency/Environmental concerns

You may also want to consider the money you may save on gasoline with a newer car. With gas prices climbing, you may want a vehicle that gets more miles to the gallon than your old one. Most new vehicles also pollute less. The new hybrid-electric car that produces fewer emissions and uses an electric battery to help protect the environment may be the perfect choice for you.

Lifestyle intangibles

Do you need a newer car for your current lifestyle? For example, were you single when you bought your old car and now you have a family? Do you own your own business now and need a bigger vehicle to run that business?

Do you care about keeping up with the Joneses or the Bickersons next door? Some people want to be seen as trendy and fashionable. If you are one of them, you may want to change cars every year or so. In some professions, such as sales, a new car every year is a sign of success.

You need to consider the intangibles and decide if they are important enough to make you purchase a newer vehicle.

The Resources

The following Websites offer more information about when to think about buying a new car:

www.cars.com

This Website contains information about how much it costs to own and operate a new car.

www.partsamerica.com/maintenanceailingcar.aspx

This Website from the auto parts company, Parts America, has a great deal of valuable information about auto accessories, repairs and maintenance.

www.kbb.com

The Kelley Blue Book Website contains a variety of information about new and used cars.

www.doityourself.com/stry/distancetips

This Website includes information about fixing up your old car and doing maintenance on your new car yourself.

2
How Much Car Can I Afford?

One of the most important factors you need to consider before you begin to research a car is to ascertain how much money you can spend to buy your new (or new-to-you) vehicle. However, you cannot forget to include such important costs as insurance, maintenance, gasoline and repairs. You need to consider two factors in your calculations: what the total cost is to own and run the car and how much you can afford to buy the car.

The Challenge

Spending What You Can Afford

Fixed Expenses vs. Flexible Costs

While you cannot know for certain how much it will cost to own your new car once you have it in your garage, there are ways to estimate the costs both manually and electronically (using the Internet). Expenses that stay the same each month are called *fixed* expenses. Expenses that change from month to month, contingent on the weather, your family's activities and the age of the car, etc. are called *flexible* expenses. No matter which method you use, you will need to estimate both fixed and flexible costs.

The chart below lists typical fixed and flexible expenses:

Car Expenses	
Fixed	**Flexible**
Down payment (one time only)	Gasoline
Monthly loan payment	Oil changes
Insurance	Tires
License fees	Maintenance
Taxes	Repairs
Other	Other

Based on these categories, you should be able to come up with a rough estimate of your gas and oil costs per month. If you buy a new car, you should not need to buy tires or have to pay for any major repairs for a few years as the warranty should cover anything major.

Internet

A faster way to figure out the complete cost of owning a car is to visit *www.edmunds.com* and use their online calculator called True Cost to Own [SM] or TCO.

This proprietary calculator allows consumers to choose a particular make, model and year of vehicle and then estimate how much that car will cost to own for the first 5 years. The calculation includes depreciation, financing, insurance, taxes and fees, gasoline, maintenance and repairs. The TCO calculator can also compare the cost to own three different cars, so consumers can see how one car may be cheaper to buy, but more expensive to own over time.

Obviously, the TCO is not a crystal ball, but you can get some excellent numbers to help you figure out your family budget amount. Edmunds.com also has calculators that will help you figure out car-financing costs and compare the various costs of buying new, buying used or leasing a car.

The Facts

The Language of Car Ownership

Before you look at your family budget and compare the costs of several vehicles, you need to understand the language of car ownership.

Interest rates

Interest is what you pay to borrow money. If interest rates are low, you can borrow money at a lower cost and consequently buy a nicer car. If interest rates are high, you will have to pay more for the money you need to buy your car which can impact the amount you can actually spend on the car itself.

Credit score

Your credit score will help determine the interest rate that you will get to buy a car. If your credit is excellent with no late payments and just a little credit card debt, you will be allowed to borrow money at the lowest possible rate at the time. However, if your credit is less than perfect, you will be charged a higher interest rate because the financing institution (bank, credit union or car dealership) considers you to be a bigger risk to default on the loan. In some cases, the bank or credit union will not qualify you for a car loan, and you will need to check with the dealership to see if they will give you a loan. If you get a loan through the dealership, they may charge you a higher interest rate.

Down Payment

When you figure out your family budget figures, make sure to include the cost of a down payment. Most banks and credit unions like consumers to put down at least 10 percent of the car price in their own money. No-money-down loans from the car dealership can cost more in interest and financing fees. Also, check to see how long it will take to pay off the car. Dealerships used to calculate routinely loans based on a 60-month term, but have begun to use a 72-month period.

Depreciation

Unlike houses or property, cars depreciate very quickly. Depreciation is the amount that the value of your car drops when you own it. For example, you may pay $23,000 for your new car, but as soon as you drive that car off the lot as the owner, the value of your car will have dropped a minimum of 20 percent to 30 percent.

As much as possible, you will want to buy a car that will not depreciate in value drastically. This is especially true if you are planning to sell your car a few years after you buy it. See Chapter 4 *Which Cars Retain the Best Resale Values?* for information about purchasing cars that have good resale value. If you chose to lease a car, then the amount it will depreciate is somewhat less important to you although it will affect your lease price.

Insurance

Insurance can be a tricky calculation because it is based on personal characteristics such as your age, credit score, driving history, marital status and where you will be parking your car. Most of the major car insurance Websites have calculators to help you figure out how much your car insurance premium would be for specific makes and models. Some of these sites are listed at the end of the chapter.

Maintenance and Repairs

Maintenance is considered to be of two types: scheduled maintenance such as oil changes or tune-ups at various mileage levels and unscheduled maintenance such as getting a new battery or wiper blades when you need them. Repairs include anything not covered by the warranty for the vehicle.

Gas and Driving Habits

The cost for gasoline is rising. However, driving habits affect fuel consumption and what is spent on gas almost as much as the price of gas. If you make frequent stops at high speed, hit the accelerator hard when the light goes to green (also called a jackrabbit start) or spend most of your miles in a large urban environment, you will use more gasoline. See Chapter 47 *How Can I Improve Gas Mileage?* on finding fuel-efficient cars and driving to conserve gas.

The Solutions

Family Budget

Using a manual method or via the Internet, calculate your take-home pay; what you actually bring home each month. Next, total your expenses for the month. Subtract expenses from income, and you will have the amount that you are able to spend on a car. Do not spend everything on the vehicle purchase. Always leave extra funds for emergencies.

In general, experts believe that you should spend about 15 percent of your monthly income on a used car payment and about 20 percent to 30 percent of your monthly income on a new car payment.

The Resources

The following Websites offer more information to help you figure out how much car you can afford:

www.nadaguides.com

The National Automobile Dealers Association (NADA) offers research and guides about figuring the costs of owning a car.

www.edmunds.com

This Website has an excellent listing of advice columns and research help. Their new search engine called True Cost to Own[SM] (TCO) is a great way to figure out how much a particular make and model will cost you over 5 years.

www.geico.com

Compare insurance rates at Geico.com and see what the car you want will cost in insurance.

Other insurance Websites you might consider for quotes include:

www.esurance.com

www.insureone.com

Which Safety Features Are Important on a New Car?

Safety devices have come a long way since Mr. Ford created the assembly line. Today's safety devices control everything from the braking systems to the vehicle's stability on the road.

The Challenge

No matter how safe new cars become, the ultimate requirement for safe driving is a safe driver. Even with all the new safety equipment, human error is still responsible for most accidents.

The Facts

Safety Ratings

Two organizations test American vehicles for safety issues and crashworthiness. They are the Insurance Institute for Highway Safety (IIHS) and the National Highway Traffic Safety Administration (NHTSA), part of the Department of Transportation. These organizations focus on the most popular vehicles and do not test all cars. For a free download of results of the *IIHS Test,* please visit: *www.encouragement press.com*

The Solutions

Glossary of Safety Features

Anti-Lock Brakes (ABS)
> This feature keeps the brakes from locking up if the driver slams down on them while in wet or slippery conditions. ABS usually prevents skids.

Air Bag Disable Switch
> This switch disables the air bag for the driver and the passenger. The feature is necessary for some people who might be more hurt by the air bag being deployed than by hitting the steering wheel or dashboard.

Back-Up Sensing System

The feature warns you when your vehicle backs up too closely to an object. This device helps prevent drivers from accidentally running over people, animals or inanimate objects and backing into a parked or moving car.

Brake Assist

This safety feature helps the driver stop more efficiently by automatically pushing harder on the brakes. Studies have shown that drivers often hesitate before hitting the brakes in an emergency. Brake assist stops the car more quickly than the driver alone.

Bumpers

Bumpers cushion the vehicle from contact with another car or a hard surface.

Child Safety Seat Tethers (LATCH)

This feature called LATCH (lower anchors and tethers for children) helps parents install their child's safety seat correctly. The straps anchor the child safety seat to the rear seat.

Crumple Zones

This feature protects the driver and passengers. Engineers designed the body panels on modern cars to crunch up in a particular pattern to absorb the impact of a collision.

Daytime Running Lights (DRL)

This new feature turns on the car's headlights automatically when the car is being driven. Statistics show that other drivers can see your car better even in daylight if you use headlights.

Electronic Brake-Force Distribution (EBD)

This system distributes the braking pressure between the front and rear brakes, taking into account the speed of the car and conditions on the road.

Electronic Stability Control (ESC), Electronic Stability System (ESS) or Vehicle Stability Control (VSC)

These systems are currently available only on high-end luxury cars, but are becoming popular with consumers. This system controls the ABS, traction controls and the way your vehicle moves from side to side to keep the car on the road.

Frontal Air Bags

These have been standard equipment on new cars since 1998. When the car is in a collision, the air bags protect the driver and passenger from hitting the steering wheel or the dashboard.

Head Restraints

Headrests were added to cars in order to prevent whiplash injuries. Some newer cars have an advanced version of the headrest that moves down and back if the car is hit from behind.

Integrated Child Booster Seats

Some minivans now include a child booster seat in the middle of the back seat. These integrated seats may not be as safe as the child booster seats purchased separately. Check to see how comfortable this optional seat is for your child before you buy the vehicle.

Night Vision Display/Technology

Cadillac has been adding this new feature as an option on their high-end vehicles. The night vision display projects the vehicle controls onto the inside of the windshield. The night vision technology allows drivers to see in front of them beyond what the headlights show.

Retractor Seatbelts (ALR/ELR)

This feature causes the seat belts to lock in place if the child safety seat or the passenger pitches forward at a particular rate of speed associated with accidents. The seat belts also tighten automatically so that parents can be sure that the child seat is installed correctly.

Safety Belts

Seat belts are one of the oldest safety features on the car. Of course, they only work if you use them. Today's safety belts include both a lap belt and a shoulder belt to protect passengers and the driver from being catapulted out of the car.

Side Air Bags (SABs)

Side air bags protect the driver and passenger in the case of a side-impact collision.

Side Curtain Airbags (Rollover Air Bags)

Curtain side air bags are now being configured to inflate in the event of a rollover. Rollover air bags will stay open longer in order to protect passengers from being ejected from the vehicle.

Tire Pressure Monitoring System (TPMS)

This system is now being phased into new car designs and should be available on all cars by 2007. This feature monitors the pressure of all four tires and alerts the driver when one or more tires are underinflated.

Traction Control

This system helps the driver maintain control while speeding up. With traction control, you will be less likely to spin your tires in loose gravel or on a wet road.

Vehicle Dynamics Integrated Management (VDIM)

This new technology takes ABS and electronic stability to another level. This system monitors the ABS, stability controls, road conditions, brakes and the other systems of the car to sense trouble before the driver is even aware of it.

Weight

Experts advise that a heavier and bigger car is usually better protection in an accident.

Family Safety Checklist

If you have a family, the NHTSA suggests that you use a checklist to compare the safety features of the vehicles you are considering. For a sample *Family Safety Checklist*, visit *www.encouragementpress.com*.

The Resources

The following Websites offer more information about safety features in new vehicles:

www.safercar.gov

The NHTSA lists all of its latest crash test and rollover ratings on this Website.

www.iihs.org

The Insurance Institute for Highway Safety (IIHS) has a Website with excellent information about safety ratings for new cars.

www.iii.org

The Insurance Information Institute (III) has information about finding safe cars and shopping for safety features.

www.kbb.com

Check out the Kelley Blue Book Website for information about safety features and ratings on all new cars.

4

Which Cars Retain the Best Resale Values?

When most people visit the new car showroom, they seldom think about reselling the car they are just about to buy. However, savvy consumers think about that seriously before they purchase a new car. If you plan to drive your car for 10 years or more, resale value is not important to you; however, if you are planning to sell your car after 3 to 5 years, you want to choose a car with good resale value. Good resale value means that you will get a good trade-in amount for your car from the dealer or will be able to sell your car to a private buyer for a tidy sum.

The Challenge

Although resale value is generally not as important to new car buyers as other considerations, it should be taken into account. Choose a car that will work well for you while you own it and sell for above average when you are ready to buy a new car.

The Facts

Not all cars are created equal. Some new car models are trendy and sporty, but they do not resell well. Remember the Gremlin and the Pacer? They are rare now because no one wanted to buy them after the initial excitement wore off in the 1970s. You do not want to buy the 2006 equivalent of the Pacer.

Best Resale Values by Class

The figures on the next page represent residual value analyses for 2006 models from the Automotive Lease Guide. Residual values help in determining prices for car leasing. Consumer buying patterns, car production levels at the manufacturer and actual car-buyer pricing are all considered in figuring a car's residual value.

Vehicles That Should Retain at Least 50 Percent of Their Value after 3 Years				
Car Class	Make & Model	Style	Residual Value	Overall Rating
Compact	Mini Cooper	Hatchback	67.3 %	1
Midsize	Mercedes-Benz E-Class	E55 sedan	61.7 %	4
Sports car	Porsche 911 Carrera	Coupe	62.9 %	2
Near luxury	BMW 325	Convertible Ci	60.4 %	Not rated
Luxury	BMW 650	Convertible i	61.3 %	6
Minivan	Honda Odyssey	LX	59.4 %	Not rated
Compact SUV	Jeep Wrangler	4x4 unlimited	58.8 %	Not rated
Midsize SUV	Land Rover LR3	SE	61.8 %	3
Full-size SUV	Toyota Sequoia	4x2 SR5	59.5 %	Not rated
Compact truck	Toyota Tacoma	4x2 access cab PreRunner	61.0 %	8
Full-size truck	Toyota Tundra	SR5 V8	60.5 %	10

Worst Resale Values

The cars below may not belong in the Gremlin category, but they do not seem to be selling well after their initial introduction.

Vehicles That May Lose as Much as 50 Percent of Their Value after 3 Years				
Overall Rating	Make & Model	Style	Car Class	Residual Value
1	Kia Rio	Sedan	Compact	24.8 %
2	Ford F-150	XL	Full-size truck	28.7 %
3	Ford Ranger	XL	Compact truck	28.8 %
4	Chevrolet Colorado	Regular cab work truck	Compact truck	29.7 %
5	Mazda B2300	4x2 regular cab	Compact truck	29.8 %
6	Isuzu Ascender	4x2 5-passenger S	Midsize SUV	30.9 %
7	Ford Taurus	SEL	Midsize sedan	31.2 %
8	Dodge Stratus	SXT	Midsize sedan	31.4 %
9	Hyundai Accent	GLS	Compact	32.2 %
10	Chevrolet Silverado 1500	Regular cab work truck	Full-size truck	32.2 %

The Solutions

If you follow the simple rules below, you can choose a new car that you like and that will sell well later on.

Choose a Popular, Well-Regarded Make and Model

You do not have to buy the most popular car in America, but it helps. If you buy a car from a carmaker who is well thought of, you should be able to recoup a nice price when you are ready to sell. If the car won any awards from *Car & Driver* or other car magazines, all the better. You can also check *Consumer Reports* to see which cars have the highest reviews for the year.

If you must buy the latest model, buy early. The sooner you buy, the sooner you can still sell it to someone else who wants to be trendy.

Do Not Choose a Bizarre or Trendy Color

Bright or bizarre paint jobs can be fun. However, it can be difficult to sell a DayGlo® orange or passion pink car in some regions. If resale value is important to you, choose a standard color on a regular car.

Choose a Car Company That Does Not Change the Body Style Every Year or Two

Experts advise that carmakers that do not change their body style frequently have cars with the best resale value. So check out the car Websites and the library to find out which manufacturers change their cars every year. Stay away from them and their wares.

Choose a Car with Popular Features Such As Air Conditioning, Stereo and Cruise Control

You can certainly sell a car with no extras at all, but most people want a car with a few bells and whistles. Some of the most common feature packages include air conditioning, a CD stereo with two or more speakers and cruise control. In sunnier climates, a sunroof or moonroof can also be an excellent selling point.

Beware of overdoing the stereo. A nice stereo is good for you as the original owner. But will the next owner pay a lot of extra money for it? Whenever you are tempted to add a new after-market feature, think about that next owner before you do anything.

If You Buy a Truck, Choose One with Power

People who buy trucks are usually interested in powerful ones. If you are going to buy a new truck, be sure to check how much the truck can tow. You may not want to tow anything, but the next owner may have a trailer. You also need to check the towing capacity so that you do not tow something too big for the engine. If you tow something too heavy, you will wear out the engine and the drive train. This will diminish the resale value of your vehicle.

Avoid Accidents

It may seem obvious, but accidents can ruin the resale value for your car. Buyers do not want to purchase a car that has been in an accident. In fact, they will search the body of your car to check for paint or parts that do not match.

Sell the Vehicle during the Proper Season

Some specialty vehicles sell better during the proper season. For example, if you live in a state with winter, a convertible will sell better in the summer. In that same chilly state, SUVs and trucks sell better in the fall and winter.

Consider Supply and Demand

The supply and demand for your car is outside your control. If the carmaker did not make many of the cars you bought, you may have many buyers for it. On the other hand, if the manufacturer made an overabundance of your model, you may have few buyers. The good news is that if you bought a good car from a reputable automaker, you will probably have plenty of buyers when you are ready to sell.

If You Buy during a Year-End Clearance, Keep Your Car Longer

Buying a car at year-end can be a good way to save money. However, it may also be a problem if you plan to sell your car in a year or two. The reason is that you may have only owned the car for a year but the model will be 2 years old. If you plan to keep the car for 3 years or more, the age issue will probably not be a problem.

The Resources

The following Websites offer more information about car resale values:

www.cars.com

This Website provides information about cars and their resale values.

www.nadaguides.com

This Website from the National Automotive Dealers Association includes information about resale values and other car information.

www.ftc.gov

The Federal Trade Commission's Website is a comprehensive site with terrific information addressing many automotive issues.

5

How Can I Keep My Car in Tip-Top Shape?

No matter how old you are, it is never too late to learn good car maintenance skills. In the old days, a relative or family friend would have shown you how to change the oil or fix a fuel pump in the family driveway. Today's automobiles are run more by computers and microchips than by gears and motors. Since very few people have the sophisticated equipment needed to diagnose or repair problems, regular maintenance is more important than ever before.

The Challenge

In these busy times, it can be difficult to keep up with your work, family and social responsibilities let alone your responsibilities to your vehicle. It is important to find the time since even the best modern cars will not run well or for long without periodic maintenance.

Winterizing Your Car

If you live in a part of the country with cold winters, you will need to winterize your car every fall before the snow comes. To save some time and money schedule winterization to coincide with an oil change.

Remember to keep two or three working ice scrapers in your car along with a shovel, a blanket and a flashlight (with spare batteries). If you are caught in a winter storm, you want to be both safe and comfortable. Keeping your cell phone fully charged and with you at all times will also be useful if you encounter severe weather conditions.

When you prepare for winter in your state, be sure to check the following parts of your vehicle:

- Tires
- Heater
- Coolant level
- Hazard flashers and other signal lights
- Battery
- Radiator
- Windshield wiper blades

The Facts

No matter how long you have owned your car, you can start immediately to take better care of it. A well-maintained car lasts longer, uses less gasoline and is safer on the road. Follow the five tips below to keep your car in tiptop shape.

Read the Manual that Comes with Your Car

This one book tells you everything you need to know about your car's maintenance schedule. For example, the prevailing wisdom 15 years ago used to be that oil changes needed to be done every 5,000 to7,000 miles. Owner's manuals in cars now suggest every 3,000 miles. Check out the manual for a list of routine check-ups and changes (oil, filter, etc.) and when they should be performed. In many cases, the warranty information on your car will also be included in the owner's manual. Be aware that if you do not maintain your car well enough, you may void the manufacturer's warranty.

Learn about Your Car

You do not need to be a gear head, but you should understand the basic information about your car and what features it has. For example, ABS stands for the antilock braking system while TCS is the traction control system. These are newer features that many cars now have. In addition, you need to know if your car is front-wheel drive, rear-wheel drive, four-wheel drive or all-wheel drive. Each of the designations specifically indicates how your car handles on wet or slippery roads. Be sure to research any term or part that you do not understand.

Clean Windows and Mirrors Often

You need to clean your headlights, windows and mirrors often to make sure that you can see other cars and the road in front of you. The importance of being able to see clearly when you are driving cannot be overemphasized. Put paper towels or clean rags in your back seat to make sure that you can clean your windshield, side windows and mirrors in any weather.

Change Oil Regularly and Save Records

Most manufacturers require regular oil changes and experts advise car owners to save the oil change records. This record of timely oil changes will prove that you kept up the vehicle in order to keep the warranty in effect and will be an excellent selling point when you decide to sell your car. In addition, use the oil recommended in your owner's manual. It will make your car run better and give you better gas mileage.

Warning Lights

Do not ignore the warning lights on your cars when they go off. Those lights indicate a problem that you need to address quickly. If a light on your dashboard begins blinking or remains on longer than it should, take your car to a mechanic immediately.

Maintaining Your Records

Retain and organize the records of the work you have done on your car. The record of your car's licensing in your city or state should be included with these documents.

In most states, license plates need to be renewed every year. You can make your life much easier if you retain this date along with all the maintenance information for your car.

Keep Track of the Renewal Dates and Information Listed Below

Vehicle Identification Number(s) (VIN(s))

Keep a copy of the VINs for all of your vehicles in a safe place. If your car is stolen, you will be ready to immediately help the police find your car.

Due Dates of City or County Stickers

Note the due date and the price of your stickers along with the information about your car's oil changes and check-ups.

Due Date of License Plates/Sticker

If you renew your license plate or license plate sticker, note the due date on your maintenance schedule. If you do not have the appropriate license or sticker on your car by the due date, you can be ticketed and fined.

The Solutions

What to Check Weekly

Most drivers inspect their vehicles before a major trip. This is a good start, but you really should check your cars over every week. A weekly check-up can help you catch problems before they become serious or cause the car to break down on the road.

National Safety Council's Weekly Checklist	
What to check	**Why?**
Tire pressure and tread wear.	The NSC advises drivers that many car accidents each year can be attributed to under- or over-inflated tires. The proper tire pressure is listed in the owner's manual. Every week, check the tire pressure on all four tires. In addition, look at the tread to make sure that the wear is even and that you have not picked up any glass.
Turn signals, head lights, tail and brake lights.	Some accidents are caused because other drivers cannot see your burned-out turn signals or brake lights. Check them every week. Changing the fuses is covered in your owner's manual.

Windshield wipers and fluid.	Check the wipers and the fluid every week. Wiper blades wear out rather quickly and you want to make sure that you can clean the windshield whenever it gets dirty.
Fluid levels, especially oil and coolant.	Check your owner's manual for how to check the oil, coolant, transmission fluid, brake fluid and power-steering fluid. Check what the car should be doing when you check these levels. For example, never check coolant when the engine has just been on.
Under the car for leaks.	Check your garage or parking space for leaks. A few drops of water from your air-conditioner is not a problem. However, if the fluid on the ground is black, brown or yellowish, you could have a serious repair issue.

What to Check Quarterly

Some systems on your car only need to be checked every 3 months or so. Visit *www.encouragementpress.com* and download the *Quartlely Car Checklist* chart to keep up on this periodic maintenance.

The Resources

The following Websites offer more information about basic maintenance techniques for your vehicle:

www.nsc.org

The National Safety Council is a not-for-profit, non-governmental agency that advocates safe operation of all equipment. Check out their Website for more maintenance tips.

www.cars.com and *www.autotrader.com*

These Websites include additional information about maintenance on used and new cars.

www1.eere.energy.gov/consumer/tips/driving.html

This Website from the U.S. Department of Energy offers maintenance tips that will keep your car in good shape and increase your gas mileage.

6

Which Options Keep Their Value?

You may not realize it, but the options you choose for your new car can greatly affect your car's resale value. While the most important choice is the car brand itself, many people cannot live without specific options even on a used car.

For this reason, you need to think carefully before you settle on options for your new car. You need to consider the region where you live, the options that are popular now and the safety features that will impress people in the future.

The Challenge

Buying a car is a tough enough job without adding option choices into the mix. However, since options can contribute significantly to your enjoyment of the car and to its future resale value, you need to consider them carefully. Of course, you should buy the options that you want and will use over the life of your car.

When picking your options, it is fairly easy to satisfy your needs and still have an eye toward the future and the resale value of your car. In general, safety features almost always fare well since most people want to protect themselves and their family. Some entertainment options such as built-in and voice-activated telephones are becoming popular again since hand-held cell phone use while driving is banned in many states.

The Facts

Option Types

Some categories of options tend to be more popular than others. For example, options that increase the comfort of the driver or the passengers are very popular. For a list of the types of options that are available, check the list below:

Comfort

- Multi-position driver's seat
- Heated seats
- Rear-window defoggers
- Multi-position passenger seats
- Heated mirrors
- Consoles to hold coins or CDs

Entertainment
- CD players with CD changers
- MP3 players or capability
- Built-in telephones
- Satellite radio
- Built-in DVD players
- Internet and email capability

Safety
- Side-impact airbags
- Rollover airbags
- Backing up alarms
- Curtain airbags
- Traction control
- Navigation and GPS systems
- Headlights that turn the high-beams on and off automatically

Power
- V-6 engine
- Four-wheel drive
- Manual transmission
- V-8 engine
- Automatic transmission

Options as Resale Value Indicators

If you add several of these kinds of options on your new car, you will be able to make more money when you sell it.

Resale Prices for Specific 2005 Options After Three Years*		
Option Name	Average MSRP for option	Value After 3 Years
Entertainment system including DVD	$1500	20-25%
Navigation system (GPS)	$1750	16-31%
Antilock brakes	$400	44-47%
Superior stereo system including one or more of the following: satellite radio, surround sound, amplifiers, CD changer, multiple speakers and MP3 capabilities.	$1000	30-50%
Moon roof	$900	43-60%
Leather upholstery	$1100	41-66%
Alloy wheels	$400	50-70%
CD changer	$300	67-75%
Power seats	$250	63-80%

*Information from the Automotive Lease Guide

Options: Which Retain Their Value and Which Do Not?

You may be surprised to find out the options that keep most of their value during resale and which do not. Sometimes it is counterintuitive. To make sure that you are choosing new car options that will pay for themselves later download the *Low vs. High Resale Options* chart found on *www.encouragementpress.com*.

The Solutions

Choose Carefully

Whether you are having your new car custom-built at the factory or finding it on the showroom floor, you will save yourself money in the long run if you choose more desirable options. The resale value of your car may seem unimportant at the time you buy the car, but you will want to get every penny you can when it is time to sell your car. In order to prevent upside-down loans–loans in which you owe more than the car is worth–you will need to keep the resale value of your car high.

Safety

Safety devices such as side-impact airbags, traction control, anti-lock brakes and back-up alarms are popular. You can always tout the safety of your vehicle to potential owners or try to sell it to a young family with small children.

Comfort

Unless you are buying a very low-end car, options that enhance the comfort of your car will increase your resale value. Air-conditioning is considered to be standard equipment these days, but the new climate-control systems allow two or more people in a vehicle to adjust the temperature in their own personal space. Other useful options are multi-position seats and leather upholstery.

Automatic Transmission

Automatic transmissions are also considered standard options. In fact, if you order a manual transmission on many sedans, not only can it cost you more when you place the order, it may make the car harder to sell. Not having an automatic transmission will limit the number of potential buyers when you resell the vehicle. The one exception to this rule is the sports car. Sport cars sell better if they have a manual transmission.

Neutral Colors

The top three car colors for years have been silver, white and black. If you buy a car in one of these colors, you should have no problem reselling it. In fact, color is so important to some people that research from Yankelovich Partners shows that an average of 39 percent of car buyers switched to a different automaker if they could not get the color that they wanted.

Stereos

Premium stereo systems are typically worth more to you than to any potential buyer. Surprisingly enough, they do not help you sell your car or enable to recoup a lot of money, but they do make the car more fun to own. Do not expect to get a huge resale value attached to your fabulous stereo. If you want a nice stereo, buy one.

Old Options are Now Standard

Remember that the cool innovations of today will be the standard features of tomorrow. For all practical purposes, the following options are standard equipment on most new cars:

- Air-conditioning
- Cruise control
- Anti-lock brakes
- Power doors and windows

Think about this when you think of the options you would like to have. Which of them will become standard?

Consider Your Region

Resale value is a regional assessment. For example, if you live in a region with wintry weather, options such as heated seats, heated mirrors and rear-window defoggers would be desirable. These same options would be significantly less useful if you sold your car in a warm-weather state such as Texas.

Of course, in Texas or Arizona, air-conditioning would be a necessity. If you were trying to sell a car without air-conditioning in that climate, you would not get much in the way of resale dollars.

The Resources

The following Websites offer more information about the huge array of options and which ones will give you a better resale value:

www.cars.com

Check out their articles about popular options. You will see how once new options become standard features.

www.aaa.com

Look at the AAA Website for information about what most people are looking for in an option package.

www.iii.org

Go to the Insurance Information Institute to find out which safety options will save you money on insurance.

What Is Car-Sharing?

The latest trend to hit urban areas is car-sharing. It works a bit like borrowing a car from a roommate or friend except that your friends, in this case, are 100 or more people you have never met.

The Challenge

Many people that live in or near a city often use public transportation or depend upon bicycles and walking to get to their destinations. However, even the most ardent walker may need a vehicle for a specific event, project or occasion.

Enter the fairly new world of car-sharing. This service has a long and interesting history in Europe where public transportation is easily available and quite cheap even in the rural areas.

Car-sharing uses the basic principles of any cooperative organization to pool resources for all the members to use. For those who do not want to spend the money to own a car or who want to make the planet greener, car-sharing is the perfect answer to a common problem in urban centers. You have a car to use when you need one, but you do not have all the common car worries such as security, buying gas, parking, digging the car out of snowdrifts or taking the car to the mechanic.

In addition, members get to drive new models of cars and often hybrid-electric cars, so they can feel good about belonging to a car-sharing network even when they are using the cars. Some car-sharing networks also include larger vehicles such as trucks and vans so that members can easily move their own furniture or even help their friends move.

The Facts

Car-Sharing Networks

Currently, most car-sharing networks are located in urban areas such as Atlanta, Los Angeles, Portland, San Diego, San Francisco, Seattle, Washington, D.C. and Chicago. However, more networks are being set up every day.

If you are interested in getting a car-share network set up in your city, contact Flexcar (a national clearinghouse of car-sharing networks) at *www.flexcar.com* and fill out their online survey.

A Short History of Car-Sharing

Car-sharing began in Switzerland in 1987 with a company called Mobility. The company started with two cars shared by 30 original members. Today, the company is the largest car-sharing enterprise in Europe with 1,000 locations, more than 2,000 vehicles and 67,000 members.

Based on the success of European car-sharing, American companies and co-ops decided to try the concept in the United States. While not as popular in the U.S. as in Europe, the idea of car-sharing has grown in popularity, especially in urban areas and among younger consumers.

Flexcar, founded in 1999, is a private car-sharing company in the U.S. So far, it has 28,000 individual car share members and 500 corporate members. The advantages of car-sharing for businesses that need to maintain a fleet of cars is obvious. Flexcar helps companies save money and earn tax credits for greener business practices.

I-GO is a not-for-profit car-sharing group based in Chicago and is loosely affiliated with the Flexcar network.

Application Fee

Most car-sharing networks ask members to pay a one-time fee to join the network. This fee is usually between $50 and $75. The fee allows the car-sharing organization to check your driving record and run a credit check.

In most cases, members have to qualify based on the following criteria:
- Aged 21 to 75
- No speeding tickets within the last 3 years
- No major driving violations within the last 5 years
- Only one or two minor traffic violations within the past 3 years
- Credit or debit card

Annual Membership Fee

Once your membership application has been approved, you pay a membership fee every year. The fee can range from $25 to $50, depending on the car-sharing network. The membership fee pays for upkeep of the cars, gasoline, insurance, snow removal, etc.

User Fees

Unlike regular rental cars, car-sharing networks include the price of gasoline in the hourly or mileage charge for their cars. Some networks charge by the hour; others charge by the mile. Some even charge a combination fee of hours and mileage. The advantage is that members can use the car for just an hour or two and only be charged for the time the car was used. Insurance on the driver is also included in every use of a car-sharing vehicle.

Flexcar offers monthly packages so that members can pay a cheaper fee the more they use the system. The monthly fees include a specific number of hours per month, and the hours do not roll over if they are not used. I-GO has a per hour charge.

How It Works

Car-sharing networks are self-service. Members reserve their cars on the Internet, go to the car in the parking area they have been assigned, use their pass card and ID number to get into the car and drive away.

At the end of the rental period, the member parks the car in the original parking lot, locks it and walks away. The car-sharing computerized network reads the mileage and hours on the car and charges the member's credit or debit card. Bills are sent out monthly with details of the member's car usage.

If the car needs gas, a gas card is included in the car, and members fill up the tank. All other maintenance is taken care of by the car-sharing network.

Extra Fees

Most car-sharing networks have rules of membership, and members will be fined for keeping a car beyond the time limit without calling or not filling up the gas tank. Members can also be credited for having a perfect car-sharing record.

Available Vehicles

One advantage of this system is that members can choose from a variety of vehicles. In the Flexcar network, members can choose from hybrid cars, sedans, pickup trucks, SUVs, minivans and sports cars. In the I-GO network, members can choose from Honda sedans and hybrids.

The Solutions

Pros and Cons of Car-sharing

While car-sharing is new in the United States, it has the potential to be a growing business in the years to come. However, car-sharing is not for everyone.

Car-sharing organizations estimate that most people who own cars use them approximately 1½ hours a day. Based on the usage of the car, they estimate that owning a car costs about $850 per month for an hourly rate of at least $20 per hour. This includes gasoline, insurance, maintenance, parking and everything else that car owners must purchase to keep their cars running.

Car-sharing networks aim to offer the use of the car without any of the problems for only $10 per hour or less. In addition, they offer a variety of cars to choose from and easy methods to reserve cars and pay for the usage charges.

Pros

Other advantages of car-sharing include the following:

- Includes everything in the usage fee;
- costs less than owning and maintaining a car;
- no worries about where to keep the car;
- no dealing with mechanics;
- no digging the car out of snowbanks;
- reduces congestion, air pollution and energy use;
- contributes to sustainable and green communities;
- different types of cars available; and
- you only pay for what you use.

Cons

Disadvantages of car-sharing include:

- Must plan ahead (loss of spontaneity);
- must park car in specific locations;
- no consistency in car choice;
- necessary to get used to a different car each time; and
- car may be unavailable when you want it.

The Resources

The following Websites offer more information about the specifics of car-sharing:

www.flexcar.com

This for-profit corporation was the first in the United States to create a car-sharing program and is currently the largest.

www.cnt.org

The Center for Neighborhood Technology (CNT) developed the I-GO car-sharing program in Chicago, Illinois.

www.igocars.org

The brainchild of the CNT (see above), I-GO in Chicago is loosely affiliated with the Flexcar program that runs in seven other urban centers. Unlike Flexcar, I-GO is a not-for-profit organization.

8

What Kind of Car Should I Buy?

The Challenge

Before you even walk into a car showroom, you need to spend some time researching and thinking about the kind of car you would like to buy. Buying a car is expensive; for most people, the only purchase larger than buying a car is buying a house. You must be prepared before you spend that kind of money. Adding to the stress of buying a car is the fact that there is no 3-day, cooling-off period. Unlike most other commercial transactions where you can back out before 3 days have elapsed, once you sign on the dotted line, that car is yours. Unless you can prove that your car has a manufacturer's defect and is a true lemon, you are stuck with it. These reasons demonstrate why you have to do your research and spend time seriously considering this major purchase.

Your Needs and Considerations

The best way to begin is to ask yourself a few questions. Use the chart below to help determine how you will use your car and what features it needs to have:

What Do You Need in A Vehicle?	
Question	**Your Answer**
What will I use the vehicle to do (grocery shopping, picking up kids, driving to visit parents, etc.)?	
How many people will need to fit in my vehicle including family, soccer team, relatives, etc.?	
Will I need this vehicle to tow a boat or camper?	
How long is my commute to work? Do I need to carpool with other people?	
Do I want a car with good gas mileage?	
Do I want a car that is more environmentally friendly, such as a hybrid?	

What safety features do I want?	
Do I prefer an automatic transmission or a manual transmission?	
Do I need a vehicle with four-wheel drive for dealing with snow, etc.? Do I live in a rural area or have a long driveway?	
Will I be transporting a large amount of cargo or people with this vehicle?	
Do I need to consider the size of car because it needs to fit in my garage, parking deck or available street parking?	
Do I need to consider someone else's needs when purchasing this vehicle (such as my spouse or partner)? Whose needs?	

Another major consideration is price. How much can you afford? The best way to begin figuring out exactly how much you can afford is to read Chapter 2 *How Much Car Can I Afford?*. This chapter will help you analyze the actual cost of the car, as well as what you can afford in a monthly payment.

Choices: New, Used or Lease?

Chapter 29 *What Do I Need to Know about Leasing a Car?* addresses the advantages and disadvantages of buying new, buying used or leasing a new car. The answer to this question is not obvious. Some of it depends on how much money you have to spend, but most of it depends on your personality. If you can do a little car maintenance yourself, or you know someone who can, a used vehicle may be right for you. If you work long hours and do not have time to bother with car maintenance or repair, buying or leasing a new car may be your best bet.

Choosing a Make and Model

If you have answered the questions above, you should know what you will use your vehicle to do, understand how much car you can afford and have decided if you want a new car, used car or leased car. At this point, you are ready for the next step–deciding which type of vehicle you want.

The chart on the following page describes the vehicle types:

Types of Vehicles	
Basic Car	**2-door or 4-door sedan or 3-door hatchback**
Station wagon	These have basically been replaced by the minivan and sport utility vehicle (SUV), but there are a few automobile manufacturers that make vehicles with some station wagon features.
Truck	Light, medium or heavy-duty.
Sport utility vehicle (SUV)	Small, medium or large.
Van	Small, medium or cargo size.
4-wheel drive	Small, medium or large. Many SUVs also have 4-wheel drive or all-wheel drive.
Luxury car	2-door, 4-door or 3-door hatch. Many luxury cars also have the features and styling of SUVs.
Sports car/convertible	2-door or 4-door.

Research

Once you have begun to narrow down the type of car you think you are interested in obtaining, you can begin your research in earnest. If you prefer books to keyboards, go to your local library and find the most recent automotive issue of *Consumer Reports* Magazine. Read up on the car makes that you are interested in buying. Look at safety figures, drivability and resale value. This information and more is also available on the Internet. Using the Websites listed at the end of this chapter, you can easily compare make, model, features and prices of all of the cars you are interested in purchasing. The Internet can also help you read about all the various manufacturers and options (called trim lines in the business). Too many consumers think that they should go to the car showroom as soon as they know what kind of car they want to buy. Do not do this. Knowledge is power when dealing with dealers or private owners. You need to find out everything you can about the model of car you want. You will still need to decide which carmaker you will choose and the options you want.

View the chart *Everything You Ever Wanted to Know about Your Future Car* on *www.encouragementpress.com*

Call the Dealership

Once you have done your research, you should have at least two or three models you would like to test drive. Do not ever buy a car over the Internet without test driving it. Call the dealership and make an appointment to test drive a car. If you do not like to haggle with sales people, call a no-haggle dealership or deal with the Internet department of the dealership. Sometimes, this department is called the fleet sales.

The Resources

The following Websites offer more information to enable you to find the right car for you:

www.nadaguides.com

The National Automobile Dealers Association (NADA) offers research and guides about new and used cars and leasing.

www.cars.com

This Website features car ads, including photographs, from private owners and dealers. You can search by make, model and year.

www.edmunds.com

This Website has an excellent listing of advice columns and research help for new cars, used cars and leased cars.

www.carfax.com

Check out this Website to get a history report on the used car that you want to buy.

www.leasesource.com

This Website offers some of the best lease deals available nationally.

www.swapalease.com

If you want to take over a short-term lease, this is the Website for you. People who want to get out of their leases will allow you to lease for a very short term, so you can see how leasing fits with your lifestyle. New lease deals are also available on this site.

9

What Is No Haggle/No Hassle Car-Buying?

For those who are too busy to shop for their car or who hate to negotiate, there is another option. No haggle/no hassle car-buying options exist. You may pay a little more than you would if you did some serious bargaining, but not only will you save yourself untold hours at the dealership, you will probably spare yourself some major stress.

The Challenge

The good news is even if you hate to argue and dislike everyone and everything associated with a dealership, you can still buy a new car. Instead of having to ask a friend or relative to go with you to buy a car, all you need to do is check out your employer, your local members-only retailer, your credit union or a Website to purchase the vehicle of your dreams. All of these options are readily available if you really hate to haggle or if you just want to save yourself some time.

You will still need to do research to make sure that the quotes you are offered are reasonable and check all your information. However, most of the angst of car-buying has been taken away by companies smart enough to understand that not everyone thinks of negotiating as an Olympic sporting event that in which they want to participate.

The Facts

Your No Haggle/No Hassle Options

If you get sick to your stomach just thinking about entering a dealership, opting for a no hassle/no haggle route is a very pleasant alternative to sitting in an office in the showroom and watching your sales rep run back and forth to the sales manager. The no hassle/no haggle options fall into the following categories:

Dealerships

Some dealerships advertise themselves as no haggle or no hassle showrooms. In this case, you would shop for a car just as you would shop for anything else. Look at the price tag and decide if you can afford it. Make sure that the dealership really means no haggling. If you have the sense that they are just using the expression as a ruse to lure you into the showroom, simply leave.

Costco and Other Members-Only Retailers

CostCo and other member-only retailers have also gone into the new car business. The advantages are that the retailer does all the negotiating and members just decide if the price is right for them. Costco has also partnered with a financial services company to offer members a good APR (annual percentage rate) on financing. Other members-only retailers have similar programs.

Car-Buying Services

If you do not have the time or the inclination to go to a dealership and work out the deal yourself, you can hire a car-buying service to buy the car for you. They do all the legwork for a fee. You tell them exactly what type of car you want with the specific options, and they come back with the best price. The advantage of this type of company is that you know where they make their money—it is the fee you pay.

Online Sites

A huge number of online sites have cropped up that offer you a price quote from the Website itself and/or a quote from dealerships with whom they have partnered. This option is good for dealers and often good for consumers. The tricky bit is figuring out how the Website makes its money. Often, they make money on the car price and that makes them one step removed from a dealership. However, if the price is a good one, you will still save without having to haggle and you will spare yourself significant aggravation.

Credit Unions and Other Associations

Credit unions have gotten into the act to provide excellent car prices as well as financing for their members. Credit unions can mobilize their membership numbers to make great deals at dealerships just as credit card companies get the best possible exchange rates on foreign currency. The key to this discount is volume. When members come to the credit union for financing, the credit union can point them to specific dealerships for good pricing. Some credit unions such as Addison Avenue are online too.

Employers

Some large employers use their clout to get good car prices for employees using the same idea as credit unions. A multi-state corporation can provide hundreds of car sales in a year.

The Solutions

How No Hassle/No Haggle Works

Each of the no hassle/no haggle operations provides good prices and no argument with a slight difference that varies from organization to organization. However, most of them work similarly to the process outlined below:

You Provide the Make and Model

Consumers still have to do a little research even at no hassle/no haggle companies. You tell the company what make and model of car you want, and the company provides you with one or more price quotes. You should have an idea about what the car will cost even before you call. Sometimes the price quote comes directly from the company itself, and sometimes it comes from a local dealership that has partnered with the company.

You Choose Options

Some companies use online forms that allow you to choose the option package that you want. Other companies just ask you via e-mail or on the telephone to explain what you want.

You Build Your Own

Some online companies such as AAA (the American Automobile Association), allow you to configure your own car right on their site. Then they search to find you the exact car or order it from the factory.

You Get Quotes from Dealers

A number of online Websites will give you quotes from local dealerships. They ask for your zip code because consumer and dealer incentives are based on geographic region. You do not have to buy from any of them, but you can call or e-mail each one to ask for the best price.

You Get Quotes from the Website

Websites such as Carsdirect.com and others will quote you their price and then give you additional quotes from local dealerships. You can compare prices and choose the one you like.

Upfront Fees

Companies that call themselves car-buying services usually charge their finder's fee upfront in the form of a price per car that they find for you.

Hidden Fees

Websites that quote you their own price have to make their money somewhere. For this reason, you need to check where the Website or company is making their profit. Obviously, dealerships, even no haggle dealerships, make their money on the price of the car, the financing and any extras that you buy. Make sure you understand in advance what your costs will be and where your money will be going.

Delivery

Car-buying services usually deliver the car to your home or office. Some

Websites will work with you to deliver the car wherever you want. This can be convenient if you are too busy to go car shopping or to stop by the dealership. As with delivery from the dealership, check the car over to make sure that it has all the options that you ordered and that it is in perfect condition. Check over the contract, as well, to make sure that no hidden fees have crept in.

The Resources

Here is more information about the specifics of no haggle/no hassle car-buying services and online resources:

www.aaa.com

The American Automobile Association (often called Triple A or AAA) offers quotes on new cars and a great deal of research information about financing and insurance.

www.edmunds.com

This Website offers top-notch research information and prices on new cars.

www.cars.com

This Website provides a huge amount of information about new cars, used cars, financing, insurance and quote services from dealers.

www.invoicedealers.com

The online car site lists quotes from dealers on new cars.

www.carsdirect.com

This Website gives you their own quotes and allows you to get dealer quotes for both new and used cars.

www.acscorp.com

American Car Buying Service asserts that it was the first online car-buying service on the Internet. They will provide you with two quotes, find the car you want and deliver it to you for a fee.

www.costcoauto.com/howworks/faqs.asp

The Costco Website includes this frequently-asked-questions document about how the program chooses cars and gets the best prices on them.

www.addisonavenue.com/content/shared/articles/buy_rental.asp

Addison Avenue is an online credit union that offers special deals to its members from Enterprise Car Sales and others. You can find both new and used cars on this site.

10

Can I Get a Good Deal from a Dealer?

Buying a new car can be very stressful. Most people dislike negotiating, especially with car dealers. The good news is that if you do your research and know what you want, you can get a fair deal on the price of your car and on the rest of the items you negotiate with the dealership.

The trick is to keep two things always in mind: 1) never relax because the dealership is always looking to make a profit on you and 2) feel free to exercise your option to get up and leave if you do not like what is happening.

The Challenge

The challenge of buying a new car is to make sure that you get the best deal on the car. Car dealers may allow you to buy the car for a better price so that they can earn more money from you by providing financing. In fact, you may provide your own financing and get a good deal on a car only to find that you have paid too much for an extra service plan or warranty. Dealers have many ways to juggle the numbers so that you will think you are getting a deal when you are actually paying more.

The Facts

New Car Terms

At the showroom, salesmen and sales managers will use a variety of terms that you need to understand. The chart on the next page lists the basics:

New Car Lingo 101	
Term	**Definition**
Invoice price (also called invoice)	This is the price that the dealer pays for the new car. However, the dealer usually pays less than this price because of manufacturer discounts, incentives, allowances and rebates.
Base price (also called base)	This is the cost of the car without options. This means that the car has only the standard features from the manufacturer and the warranty. This price is printed on the MSRP sticker in the car's window.
Money sticker price (also called MSRP—manufacturer's suggested retail price—because the MSRP is included on this sticker.	This price shows the base price along with any options that the carmaker installed and includes the manufacturer's suggested retail price for the car. Fuel economy is also listed on this sticker.
Sticker price (also called dealer's sticker price or sticker)	This price includes the MSRP price plus the price for dealer-installed options such as rust-proofing or a security system. The price also includes additional dealer profit.
	Everyone at the dealership will point to this sticker as the price of the car. Do not believe it. Savvy consumers begin from the invoice or below the invoice and negotiate from there.

The most important step in the new car, buying game is to do your research. If you know how much the dealer probably paid for the car and what other dealers are asking for the car, you are in the perfect position to negotiate. Knowledge equals negotiating power at the dealership.

The Solutions

Do Your Homework

See Chapter 2 *How Much Car Can I Afford?* to help you figure out how much you can afford to spend. Make sure that you have a price range to bargain with and that you know absolutely the top price that you can pay.

Talk to a credit union or a bank about your financing options and rates. Dealerships may try to sell you financing, but their rates are usually not as good as you would get at a credit union. Dealers may advertise low, low rates, but you need to check the fine print very carefully before you agree to anything. The best rates are only offered to people with picture-perfect credit.

Next, choose your ideal car based on how you will use it, mileage and safety. Have a list of three to five models that you are interested in. Know the options you want.

Search Online

Use the Internet to find cars with the right options for you and then do your research. Find out the car's invoice price and the MSRP by using the NADA guides (*www.nadaguides.com*). Then find out the average price that dealers are selling this car for by using a car locator such as cars.com (*www.cars.com*), Edmunds.com (*www.edmunds.com*) or autotrader.com (*www.autotrader.com*). Your negotiation room is the difference between the invoice price and the sticker price.

Test Drive the Car

The next step is to go to the dealership and test drive the car. According to the FTC, you should make sure that you drive the car on hills, on the highway and in stop-and-go city traffic. You will also want to see how it goes over railroad tracks and how it revs up to pass cars on the freeway.

Talk to the Sales Manager

After you have done the test drive, then you can go back to the dealership and start the negotiations. Many dealerships play games with consumers, and use the car salesman as a messenger back and forth with the sales manager. If you do not have time to waste, just ask to deal directly with the sales manager since she or he makes the final decision on your deal anyway.

The sales manager may try to get you to make a quick deal by saying that the car you want will be sold in the next 5 minutes or that he does not have the exact car you want on the lot. Take your time and do everything on a timetable that feels comfortable to you. You do not have to buy the car on the same day that you test drive it.

In fact, a number of experts advise you to drive the car to make sure that it is what you want and walk out. Then contact dealerships to get price quotes. If you call, ask for the fleet manager who is frequently the Internet sales guy, too. Some dealerships are happy to negotiate with consumers via e-mail for the price of the car.

Do Not Agree to Monthly Payments

In addition, if you want to ask the dealer about financing, do not ever tell the dealer what you want for a monthly payment. Talk only about the purchase price of the car. One trick to catch unwary buyers is to get them to agree to a monthly car payment before they have negotiated the price of the car. Behind that monthly payment may be a high interest rate or a loan that goes on for too long.

If you negotiate a good price on the car, the monthly payments will take care of themselves–especially if you have a good interest rate. You can ask the finance department at the dealership if they can match your rate, but do not be surprised when they cannot.

Do Not Buy an Additional Service Plan or Warranty

Dealers may also try to sell you a service plan or additional warranty for the new car you want to buy. Be careful. Make sure that their warranty or service plan covers items not covered by the carmaker's warranty. In general, those add-on packages are not worth the money.

Try Not to Trade-in Your Old Car

If you have an old car that you need to get rid of, you will get the best price by selling it outright. If you try to get a trade-in from the dealer, you may not be happy with the amount that is offered. However, if you prefer not to have to deal with all the problems of selling your old car yourself, trading it in can be an easier way to get rid of it. See Chapter 35 *How Can I Get the Best Deal for My Trade-In?*

Negotiate the Price of the Car You Want to Buy

Read the chapter on negotiations to understand how to get the best possible deal. That chapter also explains the most common tricks and traps that dealerships will use on unwary consumers.

The Resources

The following Websites offer more information about the specifics of buying a new car from a dealer:

www.nadaguides.com

The National Automobile Dealers Association (NADA) offers a good guide about buying a car from a dealership.

www.ftc.gov

The Federal Trade Commission (FTC) offers a PDF booklet called Buying a New Car that explains everything you need to know to buy a car from a dealer. The worksheet for buying a new car is excellent.

www.cars.com and *www.autodealer.com*

You can search by make, model and year on both of these Websites. Many cars also feature photographs.

11

Does Gender Matter in the Showroom?

In the new millennium, it may seem silly to discuss the treatment of women in the new car showroom. Unfortunately, there is enough bias and unequal treatment that this issue must be addressed.

The Challenge

While women run Fortune 500 companies, create their own businesses and seek political office just as men do, women are often treated like second-class citizens in the car dealership. If you find this hard to believe, just ask your female co-workers, friends or relatives.

Has she had bad experiences when she went to buy a car? Did the sales person speak to her male companion? Was she ignored by sales staff who clearly saw her standing there? Did sales people try to intimidate her or speak down to her? Did the sales staff even listen to what she said?

Sadly, this has been the experience of many women who went to buy a car. Armed with information from this chapter, you can prevent this from happening to you or someone you care about.

The Facts

Women are a group of savvy consumers with big buying clout. The figures speak for themselves:

- Women buy slightly more than 50 percent of all the new cars in America.
- Women influence approximately 85 percent of car-buying decisions.
- Women buy approximately 20 percent of new vehicles with a sticker price of $30,000 or more.

So why are most women uncomfortable in the dealer showroom? The main reasons are the sales staff and the culture of the dealership.

Be Prepared

Make sure that you treat your car purchase exactly as you would any other high-ticket item.

Do the Research
See the Chapters 8, 29, and 30 to learn about finding the right car, researching new, used or leased cars and about negotiating.

Compare Make, Models and Options
Once you know what type of car you want, compare the versions created by each carmaker. Narrow your choice to two or three before you visit the showroom.

Role-Play Your Visit to the Dealership
Before you visit a showroom, ask a friend to help you do a little role-play. Ask the friend to pretend to be the stereotypical car salesman. Tell the car dealer what you are looking for and what you want to pay. For inspiration, ask your friend to read a series of articles written by an editor at Edmunds.com who went undercover as a car salesman.

Keeping Your Sanity during the Negotiation Phase

The following chart lists a variety of actions you can take to keep sane during the 3- to 4-hour ordeal of negotiating the final price of a new car.

Sanity Advice for Negotiations	
Car-buying Problem	**Solution**
You absolutely dread going into a dealership.	Visit the car dealership at the end of the day. Experts advise not to try to test drive and buy a car in the same visit.
	If you need to do everything on the same day, visit the dealership about 45 minutes before they close. The sales staff will want to go home, and you may be able to get a good deal just because they are tired.
You feel tired, confused and hungry as the 3 hour process drones on.	Eat before you visit the showroom. Then bring a snack with you in case your energy flags while the sales staff is negotiating.
You are terrified of visiting the car showroom by yourself.	Bring a friend along to offer moral support. Experts disagree about whether or not the friend should be male. Some women have reported that the car salesmen routinely spoke to the male even when told that the car buyer was the female.
The sales person ignores you.	You can either introduce yourself, find a manager or you can leave the car lot. A dealership that allows this sort of behavior does not deserve your business.

The sales person yells at you.	No one should yell at you. If a sales person yells or laughs at you, get up and walk away. Be sure to tell the offending person why you are leaving.
The sales person tries to intimidate or browbeat you.	Sometimes again explaining what you want will help. Otherwise, you may just have to leave.
The sales person brings in another sales person called a Sales Manager to pressure you into a decision.	The other sales person is called a *closer* in the business. This person's job is to get you to sign on the dotted line. If you are not ready to do this, say so. If the sales people continue to try to pressure you, get up and leave.

The Solutions

How to Buy a New Car from a Dealership

Buying a car does not have to be an unpleasant experience. With a little preparation, you can negotiate effectively and successfully for a new car.

Bring Your Research

In particular, bring the competing prices offered by other dealerships on the Internet. Use the Internet to find the invoice price for the vehicle you want. This is supposed to be the price that the dealer pays the automaker, but dealers often get extra bonuses from the manufacturers. Ask to see the invoice and negotiate from that price. Few people pay the sticker price (also called MSRP).

Take Notes

Bring paper and pen. Write down the sales person's name and the figures that you discuss. Write down what the sales person tells you about the car. Often, this information is completely wrong which is why you need to do your research in advance.

Ask for the Sales Person's Name

When you ask for this person's name, you are showing that you are assertive. This is a good trait to demonstrate in the car showroom.

Make the Dealership Earn Your Trust

The only way to know if the dealership will treat you with respect is to visit. If you look at a variety of cars that you are interested in and test drive them, make sure you ask questions about the features, options and prices of each model.

Many sales people will point to the sticker on the car when you ask about the price. Do not fall for that. The sales staff needs you more than you need them. You can easily take your business elsewhere.

Secure Financing in Advance

In general, dealer financing is more expensive. Even if the interest rate is good, the dealer may add extra service charges to make a profit. The best plan is to get financing from your bank or credit union. Then negotiate the price of the car with the dealership. As a final step ask if the dealer can beat the rates you have already received.

Consider a No Haggle Dealership

If you have had bad experiences buying a car in the past, consider going to a no haggle dealership. You may pay a little more for the car, but you will endure less aggravation. You can also call the fleet manager (often the Internet sales person) for information.

Ask for the Price to Be Written on the Back of the Sales Person's Business Card

If you prefer to deal directly with other people (and not over the Internet), ask the sales person to write the price of the car on the back of his or her business card. One advantage of this method is that if you come back to negotiate for that car, you already have the price to begin. In addition, you can easily use that number to get a better price at another dealership.

Take the Final Contract Home to Look Over

The sales person will probably say that the dealership cannot give you the contract to take home. Make it clear that they will not make a sale unless you get to take the contract home and think about it.

The Resources

The following Website offers more information about dealing with dealership bias toward women:

www.edmunds.com/advice/buying/articles/42962/article.html

This is the URL for the article about how car sales people operate. However, Edmunds.com is a good source for general car research and comparisons.

The following Websites are also good sources for car research:

www.nadaguides.com

www.cars.com

www.carfax.com

12

What Is Dealership Lingo?

Dealerships are like nowhere else on earth. They have their own smell and their own atmosphere. Unbeknownst to most car buyers, car dealerships even have their own slang and jargon. Sales staff use this code to tell one another what the next step in the car-buying process should be for any particular customer.

The Challenge

Going to a car dealership to buy a car is a daunting task. Fortunately, you can give yourself an edge by understanding their secret language. When you wait to be approached by a member of the sales staff, you will understand what the other salesmen are saying to each another while they wait for their ups. In addition, you will be able to pronounce the name of the trickiest model or automaker without any cues from your quarterback.

The Facts

The Accent on the Right Syllable

Many Americans find foreign words and phrases difficult to figure out. This is exceptionally true in the auto industry because so many foreign manufacturers have joined the American market. You will never worry again once you check the correct pronunciation in the chart below:

Automobile Makes Pronunciation Guide to Car Makes and Models*

Spelling	*Correct Pronunciation*
Volvo	vuh-vo
Scion	see-on
Porsche	pour-sha
Jaguar	English version
	jag-you-wahr

Jaguar	American version
	jag-wahr
Isuzu	ee-sue-zoo
Hyundai	hun-day
Audi	ow-dee

Automobile Models

Spelling	*Correct Pronunciation*
Terraza	tear-ah-zah
Touareg	tour-egg
Prius	pree-us
Phaeton	faye-ton
Murano	murr-ah-no
Ion	eye-on
Cayenne	kie-anne (like the spicy pepper)

*Information from kbb.com

The Solutions

Talking like a Car Salesman

While you probably do not want to talk like a car salesman in your regular life, you do want to understand their lingo so that you can beat them at their own game. Understanding the slang of the car dealership means that you will begin to understand how car dealers and sales personnel think and work which will save you money.

The Slang of the Car Dealership

ACV *noun:* actual cash value.

beeback *noun:* A customer who comes back to buy a car after an earlier visit.

brick *noun:* To send customers home with a vehicle immediately before they can change their minds.

bump *verb:* When the GM sends the sales person back to get more money out of the client.

buyers are liars *pithet:* This is the rationalization that car sales people tell themselves to counter the belief by customers that car salesmen are liars.

buyer's remorse *noun:* This is when a buyer begins to wonder if the car deal he or she made was a good idea. This is also referred to as coming out of the ether.

croak and choke *noun*: The dealership slang for the credit life insurance and credit disability insurance that the finance manager sells to customers.

GM *noun*: This stands for general manager. This is the person who runs the dealership.

get-me-done *noun*: This is a person with iffy credit who will settle for any car at any price just to get a car financed.

laydown *noun*: This is a customer who pays whatever price the salesman gives him or her.

loaded/loading *adjective/verb*: This is related to packing. If a payment is loaded, the dealership has added a number of extra fees, services and products to the customer's bottom line.

lowball *noun*: This refers to a really low price that a salesman gives to customer who says she or he is comparing prices at other dealerships.

packed/packing *adjective/verb*: This is the practice of convincing car buyers to buy additional products and services from the dealership. The customer agrees to a specific monthly payment and then the dealership begins packing in more profit.

pounder *noun*: A profit of $1,000.

quarterback *noun*: The person customers bring with them to help negotiate a good deal at the dealership.

roach *noun*: This is what some car salesmen call customers with bad credit.

spiff *noun*: This can mean any tip or payment. Most car salesmen use the term to indicate cash changing hands among the sales staff.

spot deliver *verb*: Similar to brick. This is the process in which the car salesman asks the customer to sign the financial papers before the loan is even approved just to get the deal closed.

T.O. *verb*: Turn over. If a car salesman cannot convince you to sign on the dotted line, he or she will T.O. you to someone else.

today buyer *noun*: This is a customer who comes into the showroom specifically to buy a car. Car salesmen believe that they must turn every up into a today buyer.

up *noun*: This is a customer who walks into the dealership. Car salesmen take turns greeting walk-in customers.

voucher *noun*: The dealership lets salesmen know what their commission is with a voucher system. Until the deal is finalized, most salesmen do not know how much their commission will be.

The Resources

The following Websites offer more information about the world of car sales professionals and dealerships:

http://about.edmunds.com/advice/buying/articles/42962/page001.html

Edmunds.com sent one of its editors undercover as a car salesman. If you think you understand the jargon, you need to read this series of articles to understand the life.

www.kbb.com

The Kelley Blue Book Website has hundreds of articles about every aspect of the car-buying process.

13

How Do Car Dealers Make Money?

Most people think that car dealers make most of their money from selling cars. Actually, car dealers make money on everything they sell to consumers including warranties, extended service contracts, car add-ons, repair and financing. In addition, car dealers make money on every car by adding shipping and handling charges and getting rebates and incentives from the car manufacturers.

The Challenge

When you go to the car dealership to negotiate the price of a new car, you can be facing a losing battle. The dealership has myriad ways to make money on you. If you negotiate a good deal on a new car, they often make up that money on your trade-in. If you negotiated a good deal on a new car and on your trade-in, they can make up that money in your financing deal. Even if you are an excellent negotiator and get a good deal on your new car, your trade-in and your financing, they will try to sell you car insurance, an extended warranty or some add-ons you did not request.

Even after you have agreed to the deal, you need to read carefully the fine print on the sales contract. Many dealerships add in extras that you did not request, including security systems, fancy paint jobs, expensive stereo systems or trendy hubcaps. And even if you decline all of these extras, the dealership will make money on additional fees that they assure you are always added to every contract including shipping and handling, cleaning/detailing and even waxing. In fact, even if you resist every single extra, add-on and fee, the dealer will undoubtedly make money because it probably did not pay the full invoice price on the vehicle because of manufacturer holdbacks, incentives and rebates.

In short, never feel sorry for the dealership. If they do not make money on you, they will recoup their losses on the next guy. Since the deck can seem to be stacked in the dealership's favor, you need to know exactly how the dealer makes money. If you understand how the dealer gets paid, you will be able to negotiate the best possible deals for yourself when you need to deal with dealers.

The Facts

Sticker Price vs. Invoice Price

Most people know that dealers make money by selling cars. The most obvious profit center for dealerships is the difference between the price that the dealership pays for a car, usually called dealer invoice or just invoice, and the price listed on the car, often called sticker price or sticker.

The dealer wants you to pay sticker price. Failing that, the dealer wants you to begin your negotiations from the sticker price. The difference between the invoice price and the sticker price is usually about $1,500 to $3,000 on your average mid-sized sedan. The difference between invoice and sticker only gets wider on SUVs, vans, sports cars and luxury vehicles.

If you think you do not like to negotiate, you may change your mind when you see how much money you have to lose. If you pay sticker, you could already be giving the dealership an extra $3,000.

The numbers get worse if you finance through the dealership; you may be giving them another 2 percent or 3 percent on your financing.

On a car that costs $20,000, you have just given the dealership $400 to $600 or more. Add to that a few extra fees for shipping and handling and a nifty paint package, and you will give them an additional $500 to $250 for S&H and $250 for the paint package. If you agree to a five-speaker CD stereo instead of the plain radio in the sales contract, the dealership could charge you an extra $500.

By agreeing to an extended warranty (just an additional service contract with the dealership), you could be paying $1,000 for coverage that you already have from the manufacturer's warranty on your new car.

How Dealers Make Money on the Average Car Purchase		
Dealer Name	**Cost**	**What It Really Is**
Sticker price	$3,000	The inflated price that the dealer would like you to pay.
Financing	$600	Added percentage of profit for dealership.
Shipping & handling fees	$250	Add-on charges that you can negotiate.
Paint package	$250	Usually only wash and wax.

Stereo CD package	$500	Expensive stereo that would cost less if you added it after you bought the car.
Extended warranty	$1,000	Coverage that just duplicates the warranty from the car manufacturer.
Total	$5,600	

The total could be as much as $5,600 dollars of dealer profit over what they would normally make just for selling you a car at a fair-market value.

The Solutions

Now that you have seen how dealers make a profit at every step in the car-buying process, you can protect yourself by understanding how dealer profitability works. Read the tips below to save yourself money on a new car:

Sticker Price

Sticker price provides a nice large profit margin for the dealership. They want you to start negotiating from this price so they can make more money. You can save yourself a great deal of time and money by starting from the invoice price.

Dealer Invoice

In general, the dealer invoice price is supposed to be the price that the dealership pays to buy each car. However, the dealership almost always benefits from manufacturer incentives, rebates and holdback fees so that dealers may pay less than the invoice price to get the car. For this reason, many experts advise you to start the negotiations with a price of $500 below invoice. Make sure you actually see the invoice. Remember to research the dealer's invoice price on the Internet before you ever walk into the dealership.

Financing

Financing is another area in which the dealership can make a great deal of money because you will be paying for your car over 60 months. Before you ever consider financing with the dealership, check with your local credit union or bank. Find out the going rate so you will be able to negotiate from a position of strength with the dealer.

Trade-In

Trade-in time can make a dealer's profit margin even bigger. Before you ever visit the dealership, go online and find out what your old car is worth. In the old days, only banks and credit unions had access to a *Kelley Blue Book*. Fortunately, today it is online. Honestly consider the condition of your car and know what it is worth. The dealer cannot give you too little for your trade-in if you know its worth.

Leasing

You can get a good deal on a lease but only if you do a little research before visiting the dealership. Everything on a lease is negotiable no matter what the dealer tells you. Check out the best leasing deals online and then go to the dealership to see if they can beat the price. The dealership will gripe, but they will probably meet the price you got online.

Add-Ons and Services

Dealerships make a juicy profit on add-ons and extended warranties. Do not fall for their spiel. No matter what they say, do not buy an extended warranty if you are buying a new car. They are just duplicating coverage that you already have. Do not accept add-ons to your car. Tell the dealership that you will not pay for the add-ons and to take them off. If you tell them that the add-ons come off or the deal is off, they will ultimately cave. You may even get the add-ons for free since they are already part of the car you have selected.

The Resources

The following Websites offer more information about how car dealerships make a profit:

www.aaa.com

The American Automobile Association (also called AAA or Triple A) has a Website with a variety of information about warranties and add-on services from the dealer.

www.ftc.gov

The Federal Trade Commission (FTC) has a Website with a variety of useful information about dealer add-ons.

www.naag.org

The National Association of Attorneys General offers a Website with a variety of information for consumers including information about service contract companies or how to file a complaint.

www.bbb.org

The Better Business Bureau (BBB) is the first place to look when you are considering possible service contracts. Before you buy the policy, check the business out in case there have been complaints to the BBB.

14

How Can I Negotiate with the Dealer?

Of the top 10 things that people dread, negotiating the price of a new car is in the top five–right next to speaking in public and going to the dentist. However, if you know a little something about how dealerships make their money and you do a little online research, you can be well on your way to getting the best possible deal at the dealership. In this chapter, we will discuss the negotiation process in a dealership, what the dealership may do to trick you and what to do if you become dazed and confused.

The Challenge

As noted above, negotiating the price of a new car is daunting. The dealership deliberately does things to make it a stressful, painful process. The salesman pretends to be your friend, but he has no authority to make any decision and needs to get the sales manager's approval for every single thing. The sales manager asks what he can do to sell you a car today, as if he truly is in a hurry for your business, but he intentionally drags the negotiation on for hours. Just at the point where you are about to get up and walk away, all the problems seem to disappear, and the dealership cannot do enough to make you stay.

If you are a savvy consumer, do a little online research and read Chapter 13 *How Do Car Dealers Make Money?* on how dealers make a profit and Chapter 8 *What Kind of Car Should I Buy?* on finding a new car. You will be ready to deal with anything the dealership throws at you.

The Facts

The Negotiation Process

At a dealership, the negotiation process has distinct steps. The dealership and the sales staff will want you to do everything their way, and they will use a variety of tricks to cause you to do so.

Step One–Test Drive

The minute that you step on the lot, the dealership is trying to make you follow their script. No matter what the sales staff says, take your time doing the test drive. A test drive should take about a half hour to do it correctly.

Step Two–Negotiation

If you like the sales person who greeted you on the lot, work with that person. If you do not like that person, ask the sales manager for someone else. You do not want to work with someone who makes the whole process feel like a competition.

The dealership wants you to sit around in an office for hours while they wear you down little by little. Do not fall for it. Walk around. Bring a book or a laptop to use when the sales person goes to chat with the sales manager.

Deal with each part of the transaction separately. For example, negotiate separately for the price of the new car, the trade-in and financing. Do not ever talk monthly payment. The dealership can build in a huge amount of hidden profit if you only talk about monthly payment. Get the lowest price possible for the car. Then you can worry about monthly payments.

Step Three–Making the Deal

Before you agree to anything, make the dealership put it into writing. Verbal promises mean nothing. Tell them you want the complete price and do not believe them when they say that fees are non-negotiable. Take your time and read through all the fine print. Question every single fee from the dealership. They add those just to make more profit. Beware of additional items that you do not ask for such as snazzy rims, a security system and a fancy paint job, and make sure you do not pay for them.

Step Four–Taking Delivery of the Car

Go over the car carefully, and take your time. Make sure that everything you were promised is on the car and watch that nothing else has been added. Check for any damage, dings or problems with the vehicle and that the gas tank is full.

If You Begin to Feel Overwhelmed

If You Feel Confused, Irritated or Intimidated...	
When you have finally had enough of the dealership, the sales staff or the sales manager, take one or more of the following actions:	Get up and leave. If you are only peeved, just walk around the showroom a couple of times.
	Ask the sales manager for a new member of the sales staff.
	Ask to work directly with the sales manager.
	Tell them to fax (or mail) the sales contract to you.
	Shop for your new car on the Internet. You can negotiate the price over the telephone and come to the dealership only to test drive the car of your choice.

Dealer Tricks and Traps

Believe it or not, dealers will try every trick in the book to get you to follow their script. The list below contains the usual tricks and traps dealers use to get what they want from unsuspecting new car buyers:

Good Cop/Bad Cop

A common trick is to play good cop/bad cop with car buyers. The sales person is the good cop who is trying to get you the best possible deal. The sales manager is usually the bad cop who is trying to make you pay too much. Remember that both the sales person and the sales manager are trying to get more profit for the dealership and for themselves. Do not trust either of them.

Newbie Syndrome

Some car salesmen pretend to be brand-new so that you can help them out by buying a car from them. Do not fall for this, as it is one of the oldest tricks in the dealership's book. They probably invented this one to sell more Model Ts. The sales staff has one job and one job only—to sell you a car at the highest possible profit for the dealership. Do not forget that more profit for the dealership means more commission for the salesman.

This Is The Best We Can Do

Unless you are trying to buy the hottest new car in decades, you should not hear anyone at the dealership tell you to take the deal or leave it. If they tell you this, take them at their word and walk away. Chances are that the deal will get much better once you head for the door.

Invisible Trade-In/Lost in Space

Another ancient trick is to lose the keys to your trade-in or the trade-in itself. No matter what you do, bring an extra set of car keys with you. If the dealership tries this golden oldie, you can just drive blissfully away. The idea is that if you are stuck in the showroom, the dealership can pressure you to buy a new car at a good profit to the dealer.

Get It In Writing

An old line is that a verbal promise is not worth the paper on which it is written. You may feel the same about anything that the dealership has written down. They will tell you that it is their policy to charge extra fees, add security systems you do not want or tint every window on the lot, but every single thing in the dealership is negotiable. Do not believe anything you read in the dealership except the sales contract.

But Will You Still Love Me Tomorrow?

In a way, sales people are actors. They play upon the emotions of consumers. They may tell you that they need to sell a car today or lose their jobs. Do not feel sorry for anyone at the dealership and do not believe the theatrics of the sales staff or the sales manager.

Killing You Softly

Car dealerships are masters of nibbling you to death. One little bite here. Another little bite there. Before you know it, your excellent deal has come and gone. Do not let them nickel-and-dime you. Come into the dealership with the deal you want written down. When the sales person or the sales manager tries to change your mind, point to the paper until they get the idea.

Never forget that you can always walk away. Chances are that the deal you want will be waiting for you in a message on your answering machine.

The Resources

The following Websites offer more information about the specifics of negotiating with a dealership:

www.nadaguides.com

The National Automobile Dealers Association (NADA) provides an excellent guide about buying a car from a dealership.

www.ftc.gov

The Federal Trade Commission (FTC) offers information about every aspect of buying a car from a dealer.

www.cars.com

This Website features car ads and photographs from dealers and private owners. You can search by make, model and year.

15

What Is the Best Day, Time & Month to Buy a Car?

You have probably already heard this one at the office. The best time to buy a car is when it is rainy on a Thursday in a month ending in a consonant. Or, at least, it seems as if people need to find a crystal ball, a soothsayer and a Tarot deck to figure out when the planets are aligned correctly so that the average consumer can get a good deal at the dealership.

Actually, it is not that difficult to come up with the right day to buy a car. All you need to consider is the dealership life cycle including the period when new cars are shipped to showrooms.

The Challenge

Ask your friends and neighbors. Everyone has a cannot-miss formula for the right day to buy a car at the dealership. Some people will tell you that the weather has to be unpleasant. Others believe that a specific time of the year offers an advantage to the regular consumer. Still others swear by the specific day of the month as the most opportune moment to convince car-sales staff to give you a deal.

Experts themselves disagree as to the optimum timing of a visit to the dealership. However, most agree that knowing how the dealership operates is crucial to figuring out a good time to deal.

The Facts

Myths and Facts about Buying a Car

Car Buying Myths	
Myth	**Fact**
You can get a better deal when it is raining.	In general, this is not true. Not only will you be trudging around in the rain, but you will also be telegraphing your desperation to buy a car to the dealership.

You can get a better deal on the weekend.	Some dealers refer to the weekend as the salmon run because there are so many people mobbing the dealerships. If you want to get the dealership's attention, do not be one of the customers swimming upstream.
The phase of the moon affects car salesmen.	Maybe some people do equate car-sales personnel with werewolves, but that is just in the movies. You do not need to shop during a full moon unless you really, really want.
Going just before closing can net you a good deal.	This is also not true. Car dealerships are interested in one thing and one thing only—money. Even at the end of a long day, a car salesman will happily stay in order to sell you a car and maybe get an extra bonus for exceeding his quota for the month.
If you visit the dealership during the holiday period, you can get a fabulous deal.	This one can be true of some dealerships. Dealers know that business will slack off a little during the holiday season. Some of them are still open to dealing because they want to make a big end-of-year quota or earn extra bonuses from carmakers.

The Solutions

The Best Time to Buy a Car

Myths abound about the best time to buy a car, and the amount of snow or rain has little to do with it. In general, the best time to buy a car is when the dealership badly wants to make a goal, meet a quota or earn bonuses. However, we simple consumers have no way to know exactly when these incentives will be offered to the dealership. But we can guess.

Monday or Tuesday

If it is true that dealerships look like a salmon run on the weekends, it only makes sense to visit when the crowd has gone down. Early in the week can be a very good time to test drive the vehicle of your choice and make a deal.

According to former dealership employees, many sales contests run through the weekend and on into Monday. If the sales staff is close to a bonus, they may be quite open to cutting you a deal.

End of the Month

Sales managers normally call in their sales figures daily. They can come to dread the end of the month if their sales figures are not meeting the quotas. For this reason, shopping for a deal at the exact end of the month or a day or so before the end of the month can pay huge dividends.

Some experts advise consumers to test drive the car of their choice earlier in the month and call the sales person every week or so until late in the month.

If the sales person seems more open to your offer at the end of the month, you can surmise that a sales bonus may be in the offing.

Just Before the New Models Come Out

If you are willing to take last year's model, you can usually find excellent deals at the end of the model year. The dealership needs to get the old models off the lot so there will be room for the new models.

Experts advise consumers to buy these cars only if the consumer is planning to keep the car more than 5 years. The problem is that these cars are sold more cheaply because they are, in effect, a year old. They are brand-new, of course, but their resale value is less than a model from the current year.

When a Car Has Been Redesigned

If a good car brand is coming out with a totally new design for their vehicles, you can get a splendid deal on the model just before the update. Many car buyers will want the fancy new design, so you can usually convince the dealership to give you incentives and a good price on your trade-in if you will take the old model off their showroom floor.

When a Car Is Being Discontinued

A similar situation is when an automaker is discontinuing a particular model. You can get a cut-rate price, but experts warn that getting parts or repairs for your new car can be difficult.

When Dealerships Are Doing Poorly

If you are planning to buy a car, pay attention to the car-buying news. Are dealerships doing better than last year or worse? If dealerships are experiencing a sales slump, you can be sure that you will be a welcome sight at the dealership. Hungry car salesmen are often very reasonable during negotiations.

When You Are Ready to Buy a Car

Having said that the end of the month or of the model year is the best time to buy a car, you can honestly get a good deal at a dealership almost any day if you know what you are doing. All you need to do is your homework. Do not be afraid to use the Internet. You can negotiate from the comfort of your home over e-mail or the telephone.

The Worst Time to Buy a Car

There are a few times when you probably should not go to the dealership.

Early Spring

According to ex-dealership managers, the showrooms fill up in early spring. People are just beginning to go outside again and thoughts naturally turn to fancy new vehicles. In this environment, sales people are unlikely to deal. This is especially true if the car you want is in high demand.

When You Are Desperate

Car salesmen are trained to smell desperation from across the room. If you are shopping because your old car just gave up the ghost, you should do your negotiations over the phone or over the Internet. Car salesmen make their livings by manipulating and cajoling people. Do not give them any more ammunition than they already have.

When You Have Not Done Your Homework

If you do not know your car-buying budget, the car you want, the dealer's invoice price, your credit rating and potential financing options, you are a fruit ripe for the picking at a dealership. Unless you have money to burn, you do not want to enter the showroom unless you know exactly what you are doing.

The Resources

The following Websites offer more information about the best days, times and months to buy a car:

www.acarbuyersguide.com/car_besttime.htm

This fascinating article is written by a former sales manager of a dealership and highlights when you should buy a car.

www.insidercarsecrets.com/best_time_to_buy.html

This Website from Insider Car Secrets explains how bonuses and end-of-the-month sales goals work at the dealership.

www.scambusters.org/cars/purchase-a-car.html

The Scam Busters' Website offers interesting insight into the right day to buy a car from a dealership insider.

www.carbuyingtips.com

This Website offers tips about the best day and time to buy a car along with helpful pointers about the whole car-buying experience.

16

Are Dealer Add-ons Worth the Cost?

Dealerships have many ways to make money from you when you buy a car. The actual purchase price of the car is the least of them. Dealerships typically make most of their profit on the financing deals and extras they add to the car or offer by way of insurance.

The Challenge

The difficulty lies in deciding which extras are worth the money and which are obvious rip-offs compliments of the dealership. Some extras make sense in particular situations; but most warranties, rust-proofing and other add-ons do more for the dealer's bottom line than for your protection or peace of mind.

The Facts

While most dealership add-ons make no sense and merely add cost, even the ones with value are much cheaper if you add them yourself. Check the chart below to make sure that the dealership is not about to sell you something that you do not want on your new or used car.

Definition of Dealer Extras		
Necessary?	Name of Extra	Definition
No	Paint sealant	Experts advise that new cars do not need any extra paint sealant or paint protection. In fact, some unscrupulous dealers charge extra for paint protection when all they do is wax the car.
No	Fabric protection	If you want to add it, experts suggest that you buy fabric protector yourself and apply it. Bear in mind that there is no proof that fabric protection really keeps the upholstery cleaner for a longer period.

No	Rust-proofing	Rust-proofing is a misnomer. Nothing can keep rust away forever. All rust-proofing does is keep rust away a little longer.
		According to the Better Business Bureau, approximately 90 percent of cars made in the 1990s already come with 5-year anti-rust warranties from the manufacturer.
No	Credit life insurance/Credit disability insurance	Credit life insurance makes sure that the finance company will be paid first if you should die before you pay off your car. Credit disability insurance makes sure that the finance company will be paid if you become disabled and unable to work before you pay off your car. While both of these types of insurance may be useful, you do not have to buy either from the dealership or the finance company. Shop for a good price and coverage from your local insurance agent or independent insurance broker.

Dealer Add-Ons

In addition to warranties and insurance, dealerships also add extra features to the cars on their lot and then charge unwary consumers for them. Sometimes the dealer will say that all their cars come with this add-on from the factory. Just because the add-on is on the car does not mean that you have to pay for it or pay what the dealer claims it is worth.

Be aware of the following common dealer add-ons:

- Pin-striping
- Special paint colors
- Chrome wheels
- Deluxe floor mats
- Security systems
- Window tinting
- CD or DVD players

Tips to Avoid Paying for Add-Ons You Do Not Want

Avoiding Dealer Add-On Traps	
What to Look For	**What to Do**
Check out the dealer's sticker on the cars in the lot. This lists all the add-ons the dealer made to the original car from the factory.	Refuse to buy from dealers who automatically add extra security systems or wheels to every car in order to inflate the car's price.
Before you even visit the dealership, call to ask if the dealership has added aftermarket items to the car. Ask what has been added and how much each item costs.	Ask to be shown a car without add-ons. Purchase a car without these extras and add only the ones you want.

Ask to have the add-ons taken off the car.	The dealership probably will not do this, but you can now more easily negotiate for the car without considering the add-ons. Emphasize that you do not want them, did not ask for them and should not have to pay for them.
If you have to deal with this dealership, find the car you want and document the add-ons.	Discount the dealer's prices by half and ignore add-ons such as tinting, paint and pin-striping. Then negotiate for the price of the car based upon what you think it is worth without the unnecessary extras.

The Solutions

Extended Warranty

The term extended warranty is actually a misnomer. A true warranty is included in the price of an item. For example, new cars have a complete warranty on all parts based upon years or miles, whichever comes first. Dealers try to sell unwary consumers what amounts to an extended service contract. In many cases, you do not need this additional coverage.

However, if you are the type of person who believes in having a back-up plan, an extended service contract may be useful. Make sure you check carefully the terms and conditions of the contract. In particular, check who exactly is providing the service contract. A manufacturer's service contract usually offers the best coverage, but is typically already in force for a new car. Ensure that any service contract does not duplicate coverage from your warranty.

If the warranty is offered by a third-party or by the dealership, check with the Better Business Bureau to see if the company has had complaints lodged against it. Since many third-party companies sell policies and then go out of business, you will want to be extra careful.

No matter who offers the warranty, read the language with a fine-toothed comb, so you do not find yourself unpleasantly surprised.

Extended Warranty Tips	
If the Dealer Says This:	**You Should Do This:**
Dealer tells you that warranty can be transferred to a new owner.	Check the wording on the actual document. Many extended service contracts cannot be transferred, and some that can be require the new owner to pay an additional fee.
Dealer tells you that the finance company requires you to buy a service contract.	Check with the bank, credit union or finance company before you take the dealer's word for it. You may find it difficult to cancel a service contract once you have paid for it and you later find out that the dealer was wrong.

Dealer tells you that the service contract is expensive because of everything that is covered.	Ask for references of satisfied customers who have used the service.
Dealer tells you that service contract covers any breakdowns.	Check the actual language of the contract. If your service plan covers only breakdowns, it may not cover parts that are worn out. Many plans use this language to pay only for broken, but not worn-out parts. You want breakdown and wear-and-tear coverage.
Dealer tells you that all you have to do is pay the deductible.	Before you take the dealer's word for it, check the fine print. Do you pay a per-visit or per-repair deductible? How much is it? Will you ever get reimbursed for these? You want a per-visit deductible. If you need three things fixed, you would have to pay the deductible three times for a per-repair plan. You would only pay the deductible once if you have a per-visit plan.
Dealer tells you that you can have your car fixed anywhere with service contract.	Check the contract. Some contracts require that you get all the repairs at the dealership where you bought the policy. Other contracts become invalid if you use refurbished or salvaged parts.

The Resources

The following Websites offer more information about the specifics of warranties and add-ons from the dealer:

www.aaa.com

> The American Automobile Association (also called AAA or Triple A) has a Website with a variety of information about warranties and add-on services from the dealer.

www.ftc.gov

> The Website of the Federal Trade Commission (FTC) also has a variety of useful information about dealer add-ons.

www.naag.org

> The National Association of Attorneys General offers a Website with a variety of information for consumers including information about what to do if you want to find out about service contract companies or file a complaint.

www.bbb.org

> The Better Business Bureau (BBB) is the first place to look when you are considering possible service contracts. Before you buy the policy, check out the business in case there have been complaints to the BBB.

17

Can I Factory Order the Exact Car I Want?

If you are the sort of person who custom-orders your lunch, you may be just as picky about your automobiles. Fear not. Automakers will allow you to order the exact car you want from the factory. The only catch is that you must go through a dealership.

Many dealerships will be happy to help you, but you need to be wary. Dealers sometimes use the opportunity of ordering your car from the factory to add a number of extra charges to your total.

The Challenge

The difficulty in ordering a car from the dealership is that dealers do not like to custom-order cars. They want to sell you something on their lot. However, if you are careful and vigilant, you should be able to make even the most recalcitrant dealer do exactly as you ask.

The Facts

Choosing Popular Options

Options are a good way to increase the resale value of your car. Some of the most popular options make the car more comfortable, such as the following:

- Power locks
- Power windows
- Heated mirrors
- Climate control systems
- Remote keyless entry

Choosing Popular Colors

Believe it or not, there is a science to choosing the color for your car. In fact, experts believe that the color you choose can affect the resale value. While many people want to personalize their car with custom paint jobs, resale value is better for cars in most popular colors. Check the chart *The Most Popular Colors* at *www.encouragementpress.com* to make sure you are choosing the right color.

The Solutions

How to Order a Factory Car from the Dealership

Not all car manufacturers allow orders to the factory. Most American cars can be individually ordered, but some Asian automakers do not allow factory orders even though they build their cars in the United States.

Find a Dealer or Online Source
Find a dealer or online source that will order the car you want from the factory. Some dealers say that they will do this, but all they do is search other dealerships for the particular options you request.

Do Your Research
Make sure that you know the manufacturer's standard retail price (MSRP) and the invoice price for the basic car and all its options.

Consider Option Packages Instead of Stand-Alone Options
You can often save money by buying option packages instead of individual options.

Also, consider buying a more expensive model if it comes with the options you want as standard equipment. In most cases, buying the more expensive model with the options you want will be cheaper than adding on a number of options from the factory.

Negotiate the Price Including Destination Charges
Negotiate the price as if you were buying a car from the showroom. Make sure that you consider any potential extra charges.

Some dealerships and sales personnel will try to tell you that a car from the factory costs more. That is not true. Since you will be buying the car the moment it arrives, the dealership will actually save money because they will not have to pay to keep the car on the lot.

Make Sure to Get the Appropriate Incentives or Rebates from the Dealer
In most cases, dealerships will offer you the incentives at the time you place your order or the incentives that are available when your car is delivered. Be certain to have the dealership put the incentives that you will receive in writing.

Make Sure That Your Contract Includes the Following Clauses to Protect You:
• All of the deposit will be returned if the dealership does not deliver the exact car you ordered.

- You will not be charged more than the price listed on the contract.
- The dealer has to deliver the car you ordered by a specific due date.

If the dealership does not deliver the car that you ordered, you are entitled to all your money back. The dealership should not keep any of it. The second clause protects you in case the dealership tries to add extra charges or extra options that you did not order. The last clause makes sure that the dealership does not order your car and then sell it for more money to someone else. If the dealer does not deliver the car by the date specified, you get your money back and purchase your car elsewhere.

Pay Your Earnest Money with a Credit Card

If possible, do not pay the down payment for the car when you order it. Some dealerships will require this, but try to negotiate the issue. If you are forced to pay, no matter what the amount, make sure you use a credit card.

Some dealers will pretend that they have tried to order your car. When the car does not come in, the dealership will pretend to lose your check, forget to send it to you or tell you that you can use it to buy another car from that dealership. If the dealership tries to keep your credit card money, you can let them discuss it with your credit card company.

Watch Out for These Dealer Tricks

Sadly, many dealers will try dirty tricks to keep some or all of your money or to add extras to the car you ordered to make more profit. You need to beware of the following dastardly dealer tricks:

Dealer P Gets the Car from Dealer Q

A common trick is for the dealer to tell you that he does not need to factory-order your car. He has found the exact car you want from another dealer.

The trick is that when the car arrives from Dealer Q, there is an additional towing charge or fee, or the car is not what you ordered. If you want to give the dealership the benefit of the doubt, make sure that you have a written buyer's order which includes the VIN number of the car, the color and all the specific options. If the dealer tries to tell you that he or she cannot get the VIN number, walk away from the deal. Chances are that you are in the middle of a dealer scam.

Dealer Adds a Price Increase When You PickUp the Car

Some dealers add extra options, rust-proofing or stereos to their cars in order to make more profit. When your car arrives, they may add these additional touches and tell you that all their cars have these options. Tell them that this is not the car you ordered and walk away.

Dealer Sells Your Special Order Car to Another Customer

Once the car arrives, the dealer may find another buyer who will pay more than your contract says you will pay. In many cases, the dealer will sell the car and tell you that the special order has not come in yet. You need a deadline clause in the contract to protect you from this trick.

Dealer Says That You Have to Buy the Car He Ordered

In most states, you do not have to buy the car that you ordered. Check with your state's attorney general or go online. Dealerships know that you are not required by law to purchase the car, but they will tell you are obligated to complete the sale.

The Resources

The following Websites offer more information about ordering a car directly from the automaker:

www.nada.org

This is the Website for the National Automobile Dealers Association. They have a section to build and price a vehicle that will give you the dealer invoice price for new cars.

http://beatthecarsalesman.com/mailbag21.html

This Website includes information about how much factory-ordered cars cost the dealership.

www.naag.org

You can find the attorney general for your state on this Website. See your specific state site to find out the laws concerning buying cars that have been special-ordered from the dealership.

www.carbuyingtips.com/carintro.html

This Website helps you handle less than scrupulous dealers and their tricks.

18

Rebates...Incentives...Is One More Advantageous than the Other?

Every year car manufacturers come up with new ways to sell more new cars. They do this by offering national rebates and incentives to consumers and dealerships. If the automaker makes special offers to consumers directly, you can count on getting a deal. If the automaker gives incentives to the dealerships, the dealers get to decide how to spend them and the consumer's benefit is less assured.

The Challenge

As a consumer, you want to buy a car that meets all of your needs including the need to stay within your budget. You want to get the best possible price for the car from the dealership. If a rebate or incentive is also offered on the car you want, you should consider all the ins and outs of the offer and take it only if the car meets your other needs. Never buy a car only because it has a great incentive behind it.

The trick is trying to get the best deal in your negotiations while also getting the best deal on a special offer from the manufacturer. Some automakers allow you to choose low-interest financing direct from the manufacturer or a cash-back bonus that you can use for your down payment on the car. Other automakers will offer both a cash-back bonus and a lower interest rate on their financing package. You need to figure out which option works out best for you.

The Facts

Definitions of New Car Incentives and Rebates

At the dealership, sales people will probably use the words incentives and rebates interchangeably so you need to listen carefully to what they are actually describing. The actual incentives and rebates can be broken down into the following categories:

Reduced Financing Rate

Automakers often give consumers a reduced or zero rate of financing if the consumer buys their car. This rate may be the best deal for you, but you need to do the math first. Also, remember that, if your credit is less than perfect, you will not be able to take advantage of the reduced financing rate.

Cash Back

Sometimes automakers give consumers a cash-back bonus on particular makes and models that are not selling well. The trick is making sure that you have the correct make, model and option package to take advantage of the cash-back bonus. For most people, the best bet is to use this bonus to make a smaller down payment or to add to your down payment for a lower total car cost.

Loyalty Bonus

Some automakers give a bonus if you have bought one or more of their cars before. These bonuses depend very much on the region and the dealership.

First Car, Graduate or Military Incentives

Automakers sometimes give specific bonuses to those who are buying their first car, college graduates and military personnel.

Dealer Holdback

None of these incentives, bonuses or rebates, should be confused with something called dealer holdback. Every year, the car manufacturers return 2 percent to 3 percent of each car's invoice or MSRP price to the dealership in quarterly installments. This money is supposed to help the dealerships pay for operating costs. Dealer holdback is the reason that dealers often pay less than the invoice price for new cars.

Current Top 10 Special Offers

The chart below is a sample of the kind of incentives that manufacturers routinely offer on their cars. For specific offers in your region, check the Websites listed at the end of this chapter.

Top 10 Cash-Back Offers on 2006 Cars					
Ranking	Make	Model	Car Class	Cash Back	Percent off MSRP
1	Dodge	Ram 1500 Quad Cab (excluding SRT10)	Full-size truck	$3,500	27.79%
2	Lincoln	LS	Luxury sedan	$9,000	22.91%
3	Dodge	Durango	Full-size SUV	$3,000	21.57%
4	Ford	Freestar	Minivan	$5,000	21.14%

5	Ford	Ranger Regular Cab	Compact truck	$3,000	20.76%
6	Mercury	Grand Marquis	Full-size sedan	$5,000	20.18%
7	Dodge	Grand Caravan	Minivan	$2,500	20.00%
8	Chrysler	Town & Country LWB	Minivan	$2,500	19.82%
9	Lincoln	Town Car	Luxury sedan	$8,000	19.02%
10	Dodge	Caravan	Minivan	$2,000	18.56%

The Solutions

Low Financing or Cash Back: Which is Right For You?

You should think about two points when deciding which option to take if the manufacturer offers you the option of low financing or cash back: your credit score and the length of your loan.

Is your credit excellent? If so, you may actually qualify for the low rate of financing. However, check with local banks and credit unions first. You want the best possible APR (annual percentage rate) for the life of your loan. Make sure that the low, low financing rate offered by the automaker works with the length of loan that you want. Some of these special deals are only for 2-, 3- or 4-year loans.

If your credit is less than perfect, you may be better off going for the cash-back bonus. The general rule is that lower interest rate becomes a better option the more you borrow. Use the online calculator at Cars.com to figure out which option works best for you.

Points to Keep in Mind about Special Offers

Automaker incentives can be a great way to get a deal on your new car. They can also be very confusing. Keep the following points in mind when you are thinking about using a rebate or incentive:

Offers Differ from Region to Region and Dealer to Dealer
   Automakers offer different consumer incentives and dealer incentives in different states and regions. Check to see the specific offers being given in your local area.

Offers Constantly Change
   Many dealers list deadlines when the incentive has to be used. However, if the deadline comes and goes before you buy your car, do not worry. In many cases, the rebate is extended or even improved.

Offers Have Requirements
   In general, getting a cash-back bonus on a car depends upon the model

that you choose. You have to choose a specific make and model (or even an option package) to get the incentive. Also, some zero percent financing plans only apply to cars financed over 24, 36 or 48 months.

How to Use Special Offers in Negotiations with the Dealership

If you want to use a manufacturer's incentive at the dealership, you need to be careful about when you mention the rebate. In general, the special deals to consumers from the automaker should be in addition to the price you negotiate with the dealer.

On-Site Research

Dealers have to pay to keep the cars on their lots. If a car has been sitting on the dealer's lot for more than a month or two, the dealer may be ready to agree to a bargain in order to get the car off the inventory.

One way to figure this out is to visit a dealership after closing time and check out which makes models are on the back lot. Come back in a month and see if the same makes and models are still there. You can get an excellent deal because the dealer will want to move them.

Negotiate the Price First

Before you breathe a word about special offers, negotiate the price of the car with the dealership. Review the fine print on the contract and then announce that you will be taking the cash-back bonus or the low financing. If you have a trade-in, bring that up before you talk about the special offers.

The Resources

The following Websites offer more information about the specifics of new car rebates and incentives:

http://blogs.cars.com/kickingtires/incentives

This blog tells all about new car incentives and rebates. Check here first to see what type of rebates and incentives are available nationally for the car you want.

www.cars.com/go/advice/incentives/incentivesAll.jsp

This Website from Cars.com includes all the national incentives offered by manufacturers. These incentives change all the time, so check often to see what is being offered on the makes and models you like.

www.cars.com/go/advice/financing/calc/incentivesCalc.jsp

Also check out the cash back vs. low interest calculator at Cars.com. You can type in the numbers of your deal and the calculator will figure out which option is better.

19

Why Is the Test Drive Important?

A test drive should be like a first date. You and the car are getting to know one another. Surprisingly, some people actually allow the sales person to drive the car during the test drive. Just as you would probably not want to be the third person on a date, do not be a passenger during the test drive. You will be paying a great deal of money for the car, so you need to decide if you like it well enough to ask for the second date.

The Challenge

Buying a car is often an emotional experience. Fortunately, you can buy a car that you like and that makes sense for you. The test drive is the time to be both analytical and excited. You want to analyze how the car handles, how it feels and how it will fit into your lifestyle.

At the same time, a test drive is the time to turn the stereo up really loud and bring a tape or CD with you to test the bass boost.

The Facts

Some dealerships have very questionable business practices. By being aware of them in advance, you will spare yourself considerable aggravation and considerable expense.

Lost in Translation

Unbelievable as it may sound, in some dealerships, it is common practice to lose your driver's license when you come in for a test drive. The idea is that you are stuck there, and the sales staff can browbeat you into buying a car. One way to avoid this trick is to bring along a copy of your driver's license. Never give the dealership your original.

Quick Credit Checks

Another tactic is to make a copy of your driver's license, give you back the original and then have someone in the dealership run a credit check on you while you are taking the test drive. To make sure that this does not happen to you, you can bring along a copy of your driver's license and write on the copy that you do not authorize a credit check.

Before You Drive the Car

Before you actually drive the car, you need to walk around and look at it carefully. The idea is to find out if you want to live with this car day in and day out for a number of years.

New Car Inspection Checklist		YES	NO
Visual Inspection		**YES**	**NO**
Paint	Is the paint in good condition? Are there any scratches or dings?		
Doors	Open all the doors. Do they open easily?		
	Can you easily lean into the back seat to get something off the floor?		
Locks	Lock the doors and then unlock them. Do the locks work smoothly? Are the locks loud? Does the car have safety locks so children cannot open the doors themselves?		
Windows	Roll the windows up and down. Is it easy to work them?		
Seating		**YES**	**NO**
Passenger seat	Does the passenger seat adjust easily? Is it comfortable?		
Back seat	Is there enough legroom in the back seat? Is it comfortable to sit? Is it easy to get in and out?		
Driver's seat	Does the seat adjust easily to different positions? Does the seat tilt?		
Safety Belts		**YES**	**NO**
Driver's seat	Buckle the seat belt. Is it comfortable? Too loose? Too tight?		
Back seat	Buckle the seat belt. Is it easy to find? Is it comfortable? Too loose? Too tight?		
Comfort		**YES**	**NO**
Driver's seat	Does the driver's seat feel comfortable to you?		
Backseat	Do you have enough head and legroom?		
	Can you easily find and reach all the items on the control panel?		
	Does the seat feel too high or too low to the ground?		
	Can you reach the pedals easily?		
	Can you adjust the steering wheel easily?		
Mirrors		**YES**	**NO**
Driver's seat	Are the mirrors easy to adjust? Can you adjust the mirrors so you can see?		
Instrument Panel		**YES**	**NO**
Driver's seat	Try out the stereo? Do you like the sound? Can you get good radio reception?		
	Turn on the airconditioner? Is it loud? How quickly does the car cool off?		
	Turn on the heater? Is it loud? Does it work well?		
	Can the vents be adjusted?		
	Click the turn signal. Is it loud? Will you be able to hear it over the stereo?		

		YES	NO
	Look for the hood latch and gas latch. Are they where you expect to find them? Are they easy to open? Open the glove box. Is there room for all of your stuff? Is there a center console? Is there room for all of your stuff? Do all the gauges make sense to you? Do you understand all the fixtures and how they work?		
Lights		YES	NO
	Can you access the inside lights? Does the dome light go on when you open the car doors? Does the headlight control work? Is it easy to dim the headlights? Is it easy to turn on and off the brights? Can you find the fog lights or interior/vanity lights? Are they easy to locate?		
Trunk		YES	NO
	Does the trunk have enough room for your groceries or sports equipment? Can the back seat be adjusted to give you more trunk space if you need it? Is this maneuver obvious? Is it simple to do? Can you find the spare tire easily in the trunk?		

The Solutions

The Test Drive

The idea of the test drive is to decide if you can live with this vehicle for a long time. To find out, you will need to spend a minimum of 20 minutes driving the car yourself. You want to find out basic handling and comfort information such as the following:

- Car handling/braking
- Car steering
- Car power and acceleration
- Car ride smoothness over bumps
- Car noise level in highway and city
- Car feel

Handling

Check the car's overall handling. Do you feel as if it does what you want it to do when you want it to do so? Is the car sluggish at any point? Does it brake quickly? Check how the brakes function in a sudden stop.

Steering

Take the car to a deserted parking lot. Make every kind of turn you can think of including tight turns, wide turns, u-turns and figure eights. Turn the wheel as far as it will go. Can you make a quick u-turn? How tight is the steering radius? Do you need a lot of room to turn the car around? Try a three-point turn. Does the car feel easy to steer? Do you feel as if you have to expend a great deal of energy to get the car to turn?

Power

Make sure that you take enough time on the test drive to accelerate the car and then decelerate. Is the car hard to steer as you accelerate? Does it pass other cars easily? Do you feel you have less power when the air conditioner or heater is on?

Ride

Drive on all the various surfaces that you will face if you own the car. Drive up and down hills. Go in and out of parking spaces. Take the car on the freeway and see how well it passes other cars. Take it into stop-and-go traffic. Drive the car over railroad tracks or rough terrain. Do you get sudden jolts? Does the car rattle?

Noise

When you drive the car on the highway, listen for the road noise. Can you talk comfortably to someone in the car on the highway? Open the windows. How loud is the wind in the car? Can you hear the wind when the windows are closed? How loud is the engine?

Feel

Can you imagine yourself driving this car every day? Can you easily see out of the windshield? Can you easily see out of the mirrors? Does the car have a blind spot? Does the car feel comfortable to you? Can it accommodate the usual people you drive including your family, the little league team or your older relatives? Can it accommodate the usual objects and materials that you transport?

The Resources

The following Websites offer more information about how to inspect a new car and helpful hints on how to do a rigorous test drive:

www.autotrader.com

Provides information about test drives and inspections on new cars.

www.kbb.com

This Website from Kelley Blue Book offers tips about taking a test drive.

www.automotive.com/Buy_New/Car_Buying_Tips/car-test-drives.aspx

If you are looking for methods on how to compare vehicles on the test drive, this Website provides valuable information on what to look for.

www.carsearch.com/buy-new.html

This Website provides good test drive advice and helpful tips about the entire the car-buying process.

How Does
My Credit Score
Affect Buying a Car?

If you are planning to buy a new or used car and finance the purchase, you need to take a good look at your credit score before you begin looking at cars. If you want to qualify for a zero-percent loan or the lowest possible annual percentage rate (APR), you need to have an excellent credit record. You can get financing if your credit record is not perfect, but you will be paying a higher rate.

Think of it this way: imagine that you want borrow $20,000 to buy a new minivan for your family. If your credit is excellent, you might pay zero percent APR for a total of $20,000 or $416.66 per month for 48 months. If your credit is good, you could end up paying 6 percent APR for a 48-month loan that amounts to $22,672 for the same minivan or $493.18 per month. Finally, if your credit is bad, you could end up paying 12 percent APR for a 48-month loan that amounts to $26,544 or $553.01 per month for the same minivan.

The choice is yours.

The Challenge

Credit scores are based on complex algorithms known only to the credit reporting agencies. However, two things can improve your credit scores: good bill-paying habits and time.

No matter how bad your credit is, you can make it better by paying all your bills on time. The negative information concerning your late bill payment will drop off your credit report in 7 to 10 years.

The Facts

What Does a Credit Report Include?

Your credit report contains personal information including your name, address and telephone number. In addition, any information from public records can also be included along with any bills that you pay such as utilities, credit cards, home loans, auto loans, etc.

Personal Information
- Name
- Current and previous addresses
- Telephone number
- Date of birth
- Current and previous employers
- Spouse's name (not always included)
- Your social security number or the last four digits (for security purposes)

Credit Information
- Date account(s) opened
- Credit limit
- Loan amount
- Balance due
- Monthly payment
- Payment history (Do you pay on time? Have you ever been late or missed a payment?)
- Any co-signers or joint owners of the debt

Public Record Information
- Unpaid tax liens
- Bankruptcy information
- Unpaid child support (not all states include this information)
- Divorce

Who Can Look at Your Credit Report?

A variety of people can get access to your credit report. All they need is a legitimate business need to do so or your permission.

The following is a list of people who can look at your credit report:

- Companies who are considering giving you credit;
- landlords;
- insurance companies;
- state or local child support enforcement agencies;
- employers or potential employers (with your consent);
- companies that you already have credit with;
- agencies considering you for a government license; and
- any government agency.

| Five Myths About Your Credit Rating ||
Myth	Facts
When you finish paying off one bill, your credit score will go up at least 40 points.	A credit score takes into account many factors including how much debt you have. If you have little debt, paying off one bill may increase your score. However, if you have a great deal of debt, paying off one bill will not make a huge difference. Your score may go up but not by that much.
If you co-sign for a loan, you are not responsible for the payments.	If you co-sign on a loan, you are just as responsible for the payments as the person you signed for. If the person you co-signed for does not make the payments, your credit scores will suffer.
When you finish paying off a bill, it is removed from your credit report.	Sadly, the only thing that can remove negative information from your credit report is time. If an error was made, you can get the information taken off. But, if the information is correct, it will remain on your credit for 7 to 10 years.
You can harm your credit rating by ordering a credit report for yourself.	When you order a credit report for yourself, it is listed as a soft inquiry since you are not a credit-granting company. A hard inquiry is when a company is checking your scores in order to give you credit. If you apply for a variety of loans for a car, for example, your credit score may drop a little.
If you close accounts as you pay them off, you will improve your credit rating.	Actually, having no credit history is worse than having a bad credit history. If you close old accounts, you may be hurting your future credit by making your credit history look too short. If you want to close accounts, close the newest ones.

Warning Signs of Credit Trouble

If you pay attention to your credit, you will be able to tell when you are beginning to head for trouble with your credit report. The signs are unmistakable if you know what to look for. For these warning signs, download the table *Warning Signs of Credit Trouble* at *www.encouragementpress.com*.

The Solutions

Free Credit Reports

You can get one free credit report from all three credit reporting agencies (Experian, TransUnion and Equifax) every year. Some experts suggest that you get a free report every year and also pay for additional reports so that you can check your credit every 6 months.

Correct Inaccuracies

If you find a mistake on your credit report, you need to report the error immediately to the correct agency. You can go online and file a change at each agency's Website.

To complete your dispute, you need to have the following information ready:

- Complete name of the problem company;
- full account number of the wrong account; and
- reason the item is a mistake (for example, you already paid the account or you never applied for that account).

Paying Bills on Time

The only way to combat negative information is to counter it with positive information. You can improve your credit report by doing the following:

- Checking your credit reports from all three agencies every 6 months;
- correcting mistakes as soon as you find them;
- paying your current bills on time; and
- reducing your overall credit card debt by paying off accounts.

The Resources

The following Websites, books and other resources offer additional information about improving your credit score:

www.simpleliving.net

> *Your Money or Your Life* by Joe Dominguez and Vicki Robin is a book that can really change your life. The authors cause you to think about your money, your goals and your life in a completely new way. You can buy their book at their Website listed above.

The three credit reporting agencies:

www.equifax.com	*www.experian.com*	*www.transunion.com*
Equifax, Inc.	Experian	TransUnion LLC
800-685-1111	888-397-3742	800-888-4213

www.ftc.gov

> This Website from the Federal Trade Commission is filled with information on how to improve your credit scores.

www.making-change.org

> This Website from the Foundation for Human Development, Inc. offers calculators and success stories to explain how to improve your credit scores no matter how bad they are.

21

What Do All Those Financing Rates & Terms Mean?

Financing a car is very different than it used it be. Car manufacturers are getting involved in auto financing along with dealerships. Dealerships have begun offering very competitive rates from as many as 10 different banks. No matter what your credit rating, you can probably find a car loan to fit your needs. As always, the trick is to find exactly the right deal for you.

The Challenge

Major barriers to successful auto financing include not checking your credit reports and not researching your finance options before visiting the dealership. In any transaction with a dealership, knowledge is power. Before you even look at cars, you need to get your financing in order and find out your options. You need to do your homework and understand the financing process.

The Facts

Financing Terminology

If you go to a dealership to finance your car or you go to your local bank or credit union, you will hear many terms tossed around. Make sure that you understand what each one means before you sign a financing deal.*Administration Fees*

These are charges that some dealers and financial institutions add to pay for their overhead and documents. Before you sign anything, ask about administration fees.

Amount Financed

This is the total amount that you are borrowing to buy your car.

Annual Percentage Rate (APR)

This number is also called the finance rate or the contract rate. This is the yearly interest that you will pay to borrow the money to buy your car and is typically listed as a percentage, such as 21 percent APR.

Assignee

If you finance your car at the dealership or through the manufacturer, the dealer will sell your loan to a bank or other financial institution. The company who buys your loan is called the assignee.

Bank or Credit Union Financing

Financing is also available directly from a bank or credit union to buy your car. This is called off-site financing or direct lending at the dealership.

Co-Buyer (also called Co-signer)

People who have bad credit can sometimes get a loan if they can find a co-signer. A co-signer is a person who has a good credit rating and agrees to become the co-buyer on your loan. If you do not make your payments, the co-signer/co-buyer will be responsible for them.

Credit Application

In order to get any type of financing, you will have to fill out a credit application. The information contained in this document will help the bank or credit union decide whether to give you a loan.

Credit Insurance

This is a special type of insurance that a dealership may try to sell you when you finance your car. There are two main types: credit life insurance and credit disability insurance. The life insurance pays the balance on your car if you die. The disability insurance will make your car payments if you are unable to work.

Dealer Financing (also called On-Site Financing at the dealership)

If you get your financing at the dealership, you will be getting on-site financing. Some dealers have relationships with six to 10 banks, and they can quote you a very competitive rate if your credit scores are good.

Dealer Finance Income

This is the income that the dealership makes from financing cars. In general, a bank will charge the dealership a wholesale rate such as 5 percent APR. The dealer will mark up that rate and offer you 6.5 percent APR. The extra 1.5 percent APR is the dealer finance income. Make no mistake; dealers provide financing because they can make a nice profit at it.

Down Payment

This is the amount that you pay from your own money to buy the car. Most banks or credit unions require you to put down a certain amount or percentage of the car's price.

Finance Charge

This is the amount that borrowing the money to buy your car will cost you.

Make sure this amount is spelled out so that you know exactly how much you are paying to finance your car.

Fixed-Rate Financing

This is an APR that stays the same for the life of the loan. Auto finance rates are commonly fixed-rate programs.

Guaranteed Auto Protection (GAP)

This is insurance that pays the gap between what you owe on your car and the money you will get from insurance if your car is stolen or totaled before you pay off the loan.

Negotiated Price of the Vehicle

This is the price of the car or truck you want to buy. You need to negotiate the price of the vehicle before you discuss financing with the dealership.

Variable-Rate Financing

This type of financing has a rate that may change over the life of the loan.

What is on a Credit Application?

When you apply for a car loan, the bank, credit union or dealership will ask for and look at 13 pieces of information in order to give you a loan. Be sure to bring the proper documentation with you. A sample form, *Credit Application 101* includes a list of the 13 forms of identification you need is available for download at *www.encouragementpress.com.*

The Solutions

Three Steps to Financing

You need to approach financing just as carefully as you did choosing a car. Here are the three basic steps to getting the financing deal that you want:

Step 1: Homework

Figure out what you can afford to pay every month for a car payment. Based on what you can afford, check online to find cars in your price range. Know both the pros and cons of leasing and buying. Get your credit report and correct any wrong information.

Step 2: Comparison

Compare APR rates from three or more banks, credit unions or finance companies before you approach the dealership. If possible, get pre-approved for the loan before you go to the dealership. Remember to negotiate for your finance rate and terms just as you negotiate the price of the car.

Step 3: Buy the Car

Before you buy the car, remember that while you can get lower monthly payments by financing over a longer period, you will end up paying more in finance charges. After the contract is printed out, go over it carefully so you understand the entire finance cost of the loan. Make sure that everything you agreed to at the dealership is included on the contract. You can ask the dealership to fax it to you or let you take it home if you need more time.

The Resources

The following Websites offer more information about the specifics of financing a car:

www.aaa.com

This is a great Website for information about financing at a dealership.

www.autofinancing101.org

This Website is from the not-for-profit group called AWARE (Americans Well-Informed on Automobile Retailing Economics) and offers everything you need to know about financing a car.

www.bbb.org

The Better Business Bureau's Website contains information about fair credit and financing a car.

www.naag.org

Look on the National Association of Attorneys General Website to find out about specific state laws concerning consumer or credit protection.

22

Can I Negotiate Better Finance Rates & Terms?

Most people do not know that they can negotiate the finance rate and terms for their new car. They think that they need to accept the rate that the dealership or bank offers to them. No matter how great the APR is, ask if the bank, credit union or dealership can do better. If they say no, you still have the first rate they offered.

The Challenge

Negotiating the price of the new car, the trade-in's value and the finance terms can be an overwhelming process. This is why most people dread going to buy a new car. They never know until months later (if ever) if they got a good deal or if they were taken. For this reason, doing your homework is especially important.

The good news is that the auto manufacturers seem to be listening to opinion polls. GM and a few other automakers are beginning to change the way that dealerships list the MSRP or sticker price on the cars. In fact, GM changed the whole process of MSRP by listing a sticker price that more closely resembled the actual prices that buyers were paying in dealerships across the country. This may be too little, too late, but at least the carmakers seem to be listening.

The Facts

Avoid Upside-Down Loans

Before you get ready to negotiate your financing, you need to consider the possibility of being in an upside-down loan. An upside-down loan is one in which you owe more on your car loan than the car is worth.

For example, you buy a new car and finance it over 5 years (60 months) to make your payments lower. The final cost for the car and the financing is $25,000. After 3 years you decide to buy a newer car, but the car you bought 3 years ago is now worth $4,000 less than you owe on it. You are in an upside-down loan situation.

You can buy a new car, but the difference between the sale price of your old car and what you still owe on it will need to be folded into your new loan. Furthermore, you may still find yourself in an upside-down loan with the second car, depending on when you sell it.

Upside-Down Figures*		
Year	% of Upside-Down Buyers	Average Amount Owed Over Resale Value
2001	27 %	$3,054
2002	30 %	$3,285
2003	31 %	$3,738
2004	38 %	$4,480

* Statistics from J.D. Powers and Associates

The best way out of an upside-down loan is to keep the car until the loan is paid off or make a larger down payment on your next car.

The F&I Department at the Dealership

The financing and insurance office (F&I) at a dealership is a profit center. As more and more people search the Internet to find the best prices on new cars, dealerships have been making less and less money actually selling cars. They now make more of their profit from financing, insurance, add-ons and repair work. In fact, NADA (the National Automobile Dealers Association) found that in 2001 about 48 percent of the average dealership's profits came from the service and parts department.

Dealerships make money when they offer you a financing deal. They also make money from every insurance or warranty product they offer. When you go to talk to the financing manager, expect to be pressed to buy additional services such as the following:

- Service contracts (also called extended warranties)
- Insurance (credit, credit disability and sometimes auto, health and life)
- Rust-proofing
- Paint protection
- Fabric protection
- Automotive repair and service

That said, you can get an excellent finance rate at a dealership. You just need to be aware that you will have to negotiate for the best rate and terms just like you negotiated to get the best price for your car.

The Solutions

Negotiate the Loan Like the Price

You are not finished negotiating after you come up with a good price for your new car. You still need to negotiate the price of a trade-in as well as the terms of your financing. You cannot let your guard down until you are out of the dealership because everyone in the building is there to sell you something.

Know Your Credit Score

Because everyone in the dealership is trying to spend your money, you need to be prepared. As noted in Chapter 20, *How Does My Credit Score Affect Buying a Car?* knowing your credit score and the general state of your credit is crucial. Possessing this information enables you to know whether the rate offered to you is really appropriate for your score or a less-than-honest attempt by the dealership to make money on you.

Be Pre-Approved for the Loan

To give yourself as many options as possible, get pre-approved for a loan before you enter the dealership. You do not have to use the pre-approval if the dealership offers you a better rate, but you are then prepared to bargain for the best rate. Make the dealership meet or improve the offer you already have.

To make sure that you are getting the best rate, get three or more quotes for the auto loan. Negotiate the rates with these companies. Then get pre-approved for the one with the best rate. Remember that a longer-term loan will give you lower monthly payments but will cost you more in financing charges in the long run.

If you already have financing in your pocket, you are a cash buyer as far as the dealership is concerned. This means that you can ask for invoice price or better because you will be paying with a check from the bank or credit union.

Be Prepared for All Three Stages of Negotiations

Most car buyers are worn out by the time they finish negotiating the price of their new car. They are unpleasantly surprised when they find that they also need to negotiate the trade-in value of their old car. This leaves them almost completely defenseless when they have to meet with the F&I department manager.

The finance department will require negotiations, too. You need to say no to all the various services and warranties that they want to offer you. As noted, the extra warranties and add-ons are usually unnecessary. You also want to remember that you do not need to accept their first offer of a financing rate.

If you already have financing in your pocket, you can be immune to most of the F&I manager's charms. However, you should allow this person to quote you a rate. You already know the rate that you were quoted from the three other banks or credit unions and you lose nothing by asking the dealership if it can do better.

Read the Fine Print

No matter what the F&I manager told you or agreed to give you, you want to see it in black and white on the contract. Do not sign anything at the dealership without reading it over carefully. Some experts advise you to take the contract home to read before you agree to it. Do not allow anyone at the dealership to try to hurry you along.

Vehicle Financing Worksheet

Fill in the *Finding the Best Deal for Financing* worksheet (available as a free download at *www.encouragementpress.com*) to see which offer works the best for you and your budget. This comparison guide was created by the Federal Trade Commission and is available in their publication called *Understanding Vehicle Financing*.

The Resources

The following Websites offer more information about the specifics of negotiating your finance rate:

www.ftc.gov

The Federal Trade Commission (FTC) offers a booklet about automobile financing and an excellent financing worksheet to help you compare the rates from three different companies.

www.aaa.com

The Website for AAA (American Automobile Association) has excellent information about getting a good deal on your financing at a dealership.

www.autofinancing101.org

A not-for-profit group called AWARE (Americans Well-Informed on Automobile Retailing Economics) has a very informative Website that offers everything you need to know about financing a car.

www.bbb.org

The Better Business Bureau's Website contains important information about fair credit and financing a car.

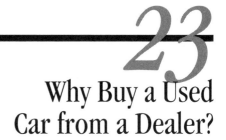

Why Buy a Used Car from a Dealer?

Buying a used car from a dealer can be the right decision for many people. Car dealers can offer some protection that private sellers cannot. This protection primarily comes from the Buyer's Guide that the dealers are required by law to post on every light-duty van, truck or car they sell and through the warranties that accompany dealer-sold used cars.

The Challenge

The challenge of buying a used car from a dealership is to make sure that you get the best deal on the car. Car dealers may allow you to buy the car for a better price so that they can earn more money from you by providing financing. Be very careful when dealing with car dealers; they have many ways to juggle the numbers so that you will think you are getting a deal when you are actually paying more.

Finding Dealers with Used Cars

The best way to find used cars these days is to search the Internet. You can use cars.com, autotrader.com or any of the many other Websites that list dealers who handle used cars.

However, if you would like to see and touch the cars in person, check to see if the dealership allows people to walk around outside when they are closed or when the sales staff has already left for the day or on Sunday. If they allow this, you will be able to choose which cars you want to test drive on your next visit without being bothered by sales personnel.

The Facts

The Used Car Rule

The Federal Trade Commission's Used Car Rule requires car dealers to post a Buyer's Guide on every used car in their lot. In most cases, motorcycles and recreational vehicles do not require such guides.

The Buyer's Guide tells you the following:

- If the car is being sold as is or with a warranty;
- if the dealer will pay a percentage of the repair costs under the warranty;
- to get all dealer promises in writing;
- to keep the Buyer's Guide after the sale;
- the major systems on the car; and
- to have the car inspected by your mechanic.

You can go to the FTC Website, www.*ftc.gov* to print a PDF booklet that includes a sample Buyer's Guide.

Certified Pre-Owned Vehicles (CPOs)

Some car dealers offer CPOs to consumers. In some cases, the dealership itself certifies the car. However, what you want is a CPO that is certified by the automaker, not the dealer. If you buy a CPO certified by a car manufacturer, you can take that car to any service center—not just the dealership where you bought it.

CPO vehicles go through a fairly rigorous process to become certified. In general, CPOs are less than 5 years old, have been driven less than 60,000 miles and have a good overall history.

In addition, these cars go through a 100- to 300-point inspection that covers the following:

- General evaluation including mirrors, lights and safety systems;
- engine evaluation including major engine systems (electrical, cooling, ignition, braking and power systems);
- exterior evaluation including doors, fenders, wheels and glass;
- interior assessment including carpet, seats, upholstery and instrument panel; and
- service and maintenance check including oil changes, repairs and tires.

If you are interested in a CPO car, be sure to get a written list of everything that is included in the warranty and make sure it is certified by the manufacturer, not just the dealership.

The Solutions

Not only do you need to know what the used car is worth and what people in your local area would pay for it, you need to know your best financing options before you ever enter the showroom.

Do Your Homework

First, figure out how much you can afford to spend. Make sure that you have a price range to bargain with the dealer and that you know absolutely the top price that you can afford to pay.

Talk to a credit union or a bank about your financing options and rates. Dealerships may try to sell you financing, but their rates are usually not as good as you would get at a credit union. Dealers may advertise low, low rates, but you need to check out the fine print before you agree to anything.

Next, choose your car based on how you will use it, mileage and safety. Have a list of three to five models that you are interested in purchasing.

Search Online

Use the Internet and the local classified section of your newspaper to find cars that you are interested in buying. Find the ones you like and then do your research on the car.

First, find out the car's retail value by using the NADA guides at *www.nadaguides. com* to find out the Blue Book value. Next learn what local buyers are paying for similar cars by using a used car locator such as cars.com or autotrader.com.

Test Drive the Car

According to the FTC, you need to make sure that you drive the car on hills, on the highway and in stop-and-go city traffic. You want to see how it goes over railroad tracks and how it revs up to pass cars on the freeway.

Find a Mechanic

Get the car carefully evaluated by your mechanic. In addition, get a car history report from a reputable online company such as carfax.com.

Talk to the Dealer

After you have done the test drive, gotten the all clear from your mechanic and received the history report, then you can go back to the dealership and start the negotiations.

The dealer will try to get you to buy the car immediately after the test drive. Do not do it. You need to have a clean history and a good report from your mechanic first. The dealer may try to tell you that the car will be sold in the next 5 minutes. Do not hurry. Chances are that the dealer has a similar car on the lot or in the back.

In addition, if you want to ask the dealer about financing, do not ever tell the dealer what you want for a monthly payment. Talk only about the purchase price of the car. One trick to catch unwary buyers is to get them to agree to a monthly car payment before they have negotiated the price of the car. Behind that monthly payment may be a high interest rate or a loan that goes on for too long.

Additional Service Plans or Warranties

Dealers may also try to sell you a service plan or additional warranty for the used car you are buying. Make sure that their warranty or service plan covers items not covered by the carmaker's warranty. In general, these add-on packages are not worth the money.

Trade-Ins

If you are already driving a used car, you will get the best price by selling it outright. However, if you prefer not to have to deal with all the problems of selling your old car yourself, trading it in can be an easier way to get rid of it. See Chapter 35 *How Can I Get the Best Deal for My Trade-In?* for information on how to trade-in your car profitably.

Negotiations

Once you have your facts, you can begin your negotiations with the dealership. The most important figure to know is what the car is worth retail and what local buyers have been paying for similar cars. Continue to fend off the dealer's attempts to sell you a financing package, extra warranties and additional service plans and negotiate the best price for the car itself. See Chapter 14 *How Can I Negotiate with the Dealer?* on negotiations to understand how to get the best possible deal.

The Resources

The following Websites offer more information about the specifics of buying a used car from a dealer:

www.nadaguides.com

> The National Automobile Dealers Association (NADA) offers a good guide about buying a car from a dealership.

www.ftc.gov

> The Federal Trade Commission (FTC) offers a PDF booklet called *Buying a Used Car* that explains everything you need to know to buy a car from a dealer.

www.cars.com

> This Website features car ads from dealers and private owners. You can search by make, model and year. Many cars also feature photographs.

www.carfax.com

> Check out this Website to get a history report on the used car that you want to buy even if the car dealer offers you a car history. The peace of mind will be worth the extra money.

24

Why Buy a Used Car from a Private Seller?

If you decide that buying a used car is the right choice for you, you can buy from a rental or repo company, a dealer or a private owner. Buying from any of these sellers has its own set of pitfalls; you need to find the used-car seller that works best for you.

The Challenge

Many people prefer buying a used car since it is cheaper and because new cars lose so much value the instant you drive them off the lot. When it comes to buying used cars, some people have success buying from friends and family. Other used car sources include the Internet and traditional newspaper ads. The trick is to find a car that you like, ascertain its condition and finally negotiate a price you can afford.

Finding Used Cars

The classified pages in the local newspaper along with free newspapers that list cars for sale used to be the best source for used cars. With the advent of the Internet, you can find used cars at a number of online sites including cars.com, autotrader.com or by placing the words used car in any number of search engines such as google.com, yahoo.com or ask.com in addition to the print media used prior to the the Internet..

The Facts

Ten questions to ask private sellers

1. Do you own this car?

    Make sure that the person who is selling the car actually owns the car. Consumer fraud with mortgages and car sales have become commonplace.

2. Why are you selling the car?

    You always want to know why the seller wants to get rid of a vehicle. In most cases, the seller just bought a new car and wants to sell the old one. Some sellers may tell you that the car needs expensive repairs and the sellers cannot afford them. Beware of sellers who tell you that they can no longer afford the payments. If they cannot afford to make their car payment, they probably did not do any maintenance or repair on the car either.

3. How long have you owned the car?

The best possible answer is that the owner bought the car new and has owned it ever since. The more owners a car has had, the less likely it is that all of them took good care of the car. With multiple owners, it is also unlikely that you will be able to see the car's repair and maintenance history.

4. What systems or parts have you replaced?

Listen carefully to the answer. If the car has only a few thousand miles, you do not want to hear that the whole transmission has already been replaced. Similarly, do not believe that a car with 100,000 miles on it has not yet had any major repairs.

5. Can I see the repair and maintenance records for the car?

Trustworthy sellers will probably have gathered them for you to see. However, some sellers are less than organized about their cars and their lives. A car with a meticulous service record is always a better buy because you know that the owner took good care of the vehicle.

6. What do you think the car will need in the next 5,000 to 10,000 miles?

If the seller has owned the car for more than a few years, she or he should have a good idea about what parts of the car are likely to need repairs.

7. Was the car driven more on the highway or in the city?

Highway miles offer less wear and tear on a car than city miles. Even if the car has high mileage, it can still be a good buy and a good car if most of the miles have been driven on the highway. Of course, the one problem with this question is that the answer cannot really be verified.

8. Did this car ever tow anything such as a boat or trailer?

Many people use their regular cars to tow things. This puts an extra drag on the car's engine, and most modern sedans were not made to tow boats or trailers. If the seller has a truck, van or SUV, ask specifically about what exactly was towed and how big the item was.

9. May I have my mechanic look over this car?

Asking this question is almost a formality since you must have a mechanic look over the car before you buy it. Ideally, your mechanic would come over with you to look at the car. However, if you like what you see, make arrangements with the seller to have your mechanic look over the car before you buy.

10. Can I see the VIN number so I can do an online history check?

No matter what the seller says, you will want to do a history check on the car. Copy down the vehicle identification number (VIN) yourself from the front driver's side windshield of the car. Do not let the seller read the number to you or give you the VIN number. You want to make sure that you are checking the correct VIN. An online car history from Carfax or another service can give you peace of mind about your purchase. You will find out if the car has been in any accidents, if it was salvaged and if the seller really owns the car.

Beware of Curbsiders

Sometimes a private owner is really just a small-time dealer in disguise. A curbsider is a person who pretends to be the private owner of a car in order to sell the car to a consumer. Because the curbsider is pretending to be a private owner, he or she does not have to comply with all the regulations that normally apply to dealers.

Curbsiders often use tall tales to sell their cars. A common curbsider ruse is to tell buyers that he is moving out of state, getting a divorce or selling the car for his little old lady aunt who died. They pretend that they really need the money quickly and will pressure buyers into thinking that the car will be sold in an hour to someone else.

If the deal seems too good to be true or the seller is in a hurry to sell the car immediately for cash, walk away from the deal. If the seller will not let you see the VIN or take the car to your mechanic, also walk away. In all these cases, she or he is probably a curbsider.

The Solutions

If you follow the guidelines below, you will be able to find the car you want and buy it for a price you can afford:

Do Your Groundwork

First, figure out how much you can afford to spend. Make sure that you have a price range to bargain with the private owner and that you know absolutely the top price that you can afford to pay. If you need to finance the purchase, get the loan in advance so that you can quickly buy the car you want.

Search Online

Use the Internet and the local classified section of your newspaper to find cars that you are interested in purchasing and do the necessary research.

Find out the car's retail value by using the NADA guides (www.nadaguides.com) to find out the Blue Book value. To find out what local buyers are actually paying for comparable cars, use a used car locator such as cars.com or autotrader.com.

Test Drive the Car

Call the owner and make an appointment to test drive the car. According to the FTC, you need to make sure that you drive the car on hills, on the highway and in stop-and-go city traffic. Check the car in all types of terrain and conditions paying attention to the smoothness of the ride and the power of the engine.

Checking Further

Make sure that your mechanic looks over the car before you buy it and you get a car-history report from a reputable online company.

After you have done the test drive, gotten the all clear from your mechanic, received your history report and read Chapter 28 *How Should I Negotiate with a Private Seller?* on negotiations, contact the seller to begin your negotiations to buy the car.

The Resources

The following Websites offer more information about the specifics of buying a used car from a private owner:

www.ftc.gov

> The Federal Trade Commission (FTC) offers a PDF booklet called *Buying a Used Car* that explains everything you need to know to buy a car from a private owner.

www.cars.com

> This Website features car ads from both private owners and dealers with wonderful searching capabilities.

www.carfax.com

> Do not forget to get a history report on any used car you are considering purchasing.

25

What Do I Need to Know about Used Cars Auctions?

The best way to hear about an auto auction (and there are many) is from the agency that is selling the cars. You do not have to subscribe to a special newsletter or go to an auction Website that charges a monthly fee. You can find everything you need to buy government surplus automobiles, other vehicles and other personal property directly from the government agencies that sell them.

This chapter will tell you how to find out where auctions are held, which agency is hosting them and how to buy your next car directly from Uncle Sam.

The Challenge

Offers that seem too good to be true are just that–too good to believe. Many online sites offer to sell guides about local and national car auctions for repossessed vehicles or vehicles impounded by the police. Many of these Websites are trying to pull a bait and switch on unwary buyers.

While it is true that the government sells a variety of cars, other vehicles (including trucks, SUVs and airplanes) and personal property (jewelry and other items) every week, the fact is that Uncle Sam expects a fair price for all his merchandise. No matter what you read in the newspaper or hear on the radio, the government is not selling like new used cars for $500.

Any car that sells for $500 at a car auction is probably in need of serious repair. All vehicles (in fact all property) sold at auction–the government's auction or anyone else's–are sold as is. This means that the buyer needs to be wary. The car could look fine on the outside but have serious flaws. If you do not know much about cars, do not try to buy a car at auction unless you have a very knowledgeable friend.

The Facts

Car Auction Tips

The Merchandise

Cars and other vehicles that the government auctions off come from one of three sources. The first source is government surplus. If the government cannot use the items or give them away, they sell them to the public. Most of the items from the U.S. General Services Administration (GSA) are surplus.

The second source is property that is seized by law enforcement agencies. Most of this property is taken because of trade violations, trademark or copyright infringement, smuggling, drug trafficking, mail fraud or other illegal activities.

The third source is general order merchandise. These items have been abandoned at ports of entry or the taxes were not paid on them.

Eligibility

If you want to bid on government auctions, you usually need to fill out a bidder registration form. Each government agency uses a slightly different form, but all have the same conditions:

- You must be 18 years of age or older;
- you must not be an employee of the federal government;
- you must not be a family member of an employee of the federal government;
- you must not represent the person the property was seized from; and
- you must not be disbarred from being a government contractor.

Inspection of Property

In every auction, the government is selling the property as is which means that the government is not responsible for any problems with the cars or other vehicles. Although each government agency may list information about the items online or via a newsletter, the government expects each bidder to personally inspect the property.

All government agencies allow an inspection period of a few days to a few weeks, depending on what items are to be sold. Real estate is allowed a longer time while cars and other personal property are usually only available for a few days.

Bidding

When you register as a bidder, the government (or a third-party company working for the government) will assign you a bidder number. Some agencies sell all of their property on the Internet. Other agencies offer both online and in-person auctions. A few agencies offer written or sealed bids for their property. Each agency listed at the end of this chapter has a complete listing of policies and procedures on their Webpage.

It is important to realize that all sales are final at a car auction. If the auctioneer accepts your bid, you are responsible to pay for the property. You cannot reconsider after you have won the auction. For this reason, be absolutely certain what property you want and how much you are willing to pay for it.

Deposits

Each sale is different, but most auctions require the winning bidders to immediately pay a deposit on their purchase and pay the remainder within 24 to 48 hours. For large item purchases, some agencies will close the deal within 30 days. Other agencies only require a deposit from the highest and second-highest bidders. The deposit amounts are listed in the sale flyers for each auction.

Payment

Most government agencies and third-party companies require that bidders pay in cash, cashiers check/certified check or credit cards. Letters of credit or corporate checks are not accepted.

Each sale flyer will indicate how payment is handled, what kind of deposit is required and when the final amounts are due. Some agencies will allow wire transfers to pay for the rest of the item after the deposit is made in cash or cashier's check.

In general, items sold for $5,000 or less are paid for immediately. Items that cost more than $5,000 require a deposit of $5,000 with the rest of the price due at the time listed in the sale information.

Taxes

In most states, buyers are responsible for all federal, state and local taxes on the items they purchase.

The Solutions

Government Car Auctions

Car auctions from the U.S. government are hosted every day. Check at each agency's Website to find local sales near you.

Local Law Enforcement Car Auctions

Go to your state government's Website and search for sales. Chances are that your local law enforcement personnel will have their own car auctions and will list all the appropriate information on their Website.

If you cannot find a Website, call the local law enforcement non-emergency number and ask for information.

Imposter Auctions

A popular scam is to list a non-governmental auction with a semi-official name. The U.S. Customs Service Website warns about imposter auctions. Auctions from the government will include the appropriate logo or seal for the branch of government and very clear information.

If you are not sure about the auction, check the Website out with the Better Business Bureau.

Non-Governmental Auctions

Anyone can host a car auction, and many are listed in the classified section of your local newspaper. Car dealer auctions are usually listed as such because the public is not allowed to bid. However, a number of unscrupulous auction operators may allow the public in even though they cannot bid.

Also, beware of auctions that require a fee to participate. Auctions at government agencies are free to the public. Anyone who meets the requirements can register to bid at no cost.

The Resources

The following Websites offer more information about the specifics of buying a used car at auction:

www.treas.gov/auctions/customs

This Website from the U.S. Customs Service lists everything you need to know about auctions from this government agency. They also offer an email update list and a yearly e-mail subscription to all national auctions for $25 per year.

www.pueblo.gsa.gov

The Federal Citizen Information Center (FCIC) is the information hub for the entire federal government. If you need to know which federal agencies are selling what property, the FCIC Website is a good place to start your search.

www.usdoj.gov/marshals

This Website from the U.S. Marshals Service (USMS) in the Department of Justice includes a variety of items that are offered at auction to the public. The USMS offers property for sale that has been forfeited to the Drug Enforcement Administration, the Federal Bureau of Investigation, the Immigration and Naturalization Service, and the Bureau of Alcohol, Tobacco and Firearms.

26

Demo, Program, Fleet, Rental, Repossessed– What's the Difference?

Many people rave about the deals they got buying demo, company, fleet, rental and repossessed cars. You too can reap the benefits of these types of used cars if you follow the tips below.

The Challenge

The difficulty with any used car is knowing how well the car was taken care of by the owner. Was the oil changed on time? Did the car receive routine maintenance? Were any repairs made promptly? Was the car in an accident?

If you are careful and can find the answers to all of these questions, you can find an excellent bargain that will provide transportation for years to come.

The Facts

Glossary of Used Car and Fleet Terminology

Cars that fall into the demo-fleet-company-repossessed car categories go by a variety of different names. To make sure that you know what you are buying, learn the terms in the list below:

Company Car
> A company car is usually a new car that was bought by a company for their fleet of vehicles or owned by a single executive as a company car. These cars are also called executive cars.

Demonstrator or Demo
> A demonstrator or demo car is a new car at a dealership that was driven by sales staff, the sales manager or the dealership owner. Although these cars are technically new, they often have more than 5,000 miles on them.

Fleet Car
> A fleet vehicle can be one of a number of types of cars, depending on the state where the car is registered. A fleet car can be any of the following:

- A car owned as part of a fleet of vehicles by a company;
- a car owned by a rental company;
- a company or executive car;
- a car leased by a bank or credit union for an individual; or
- a car from a dealership that shows up at an auction.

High-Mileage Car

These are vehicles that may be fleet, demo or program cars that have 50,000 to 75,000 miles even though they are only 1 or 2 years old. A high-mileage car can be a good value; you are getting a newer car but paying less because of all the miles.

Orphan Car

An orphan car is a vehicle that is no longer made or sold in the United States but is still made in other countries. This makes it much harder to find parts or service for these cars. Orphan cars include Citroen, Peugeot, Fiat and Alfa Romeo.

Program Car

A program car can be just about any type of fleet, demo, company or rental car. In the strictest sense, a program car is a car owned by the carmaker and given to an automotive executive to drive. At about 5,000 miles, the automaker usually sells the car and gives the executive a new one. However, the term can be applied to almost any used car including a car turned in after a lease.

Rental Car

Rental cars end up at auctions and lots after only a year or two of use. Some experts tout these cars as good values. If you want to consider a rental car, you need to check carefully the mileage, get a mechanic to look it over and buy a history report for the vehicle.

Repossessed Car

Most experts advise consumers not to buy repossessed cars. Although the prices can be deeply discounted, the cars are often in bad shape. Common sense should tell you that someone who could not afford to make his or her car payments probably did not have the money to do oil changes and routine maintenance either.

Salvage Car

A salvage car is a car that has been damaged so much that it would cost more to fix the car than to total it, so the insurance company gets a salvage title and sells it to a salvage company for parts. Some salvage cars are purchased by body shops and rebuilt. Unless you know a great deal about automobiles, salvage cars are a risky proposition.

Where to Buy Demo, Fleet, Company and Repossessed Cars

It is not difficult to find program cars to purchase. For a list of venues where these types of cars can be found, visit *www.encouragementpress.com*.

The Solutions

Information You Must Know about the Car

Before you consider buying any type of program car you need to find out the following information about the vehicle:

Mileage

The mileage is critical for telling you how much life is left in the vehicle you want to purchase.

Age

The age of the car will tell you if the mileage for that particular car is really high or low. Age is not as important as mileage unless your goal is to drive the car for a year or so and then sell it. Do not forget that when you are buying a program car, since it is already a year old, it will have depreciated considerably.

Maintenance Records

Besides mileage, one of the most important factors in considering a used car is the maintenance record. You will want to make sure that the car had oil changes and routine maintenance exactly when required by the warranty and the owner's manual.

Car History Report

No matter what the seller tells you, buy a car history report for any used car you are considering. The vehicle report will tell you if the car is salvaged, if it was in an accident or if it came from a flood-ravaged state.

Original Driver(s)

In general, cars driven by just one person are in better condition than rental cars that have been driven by many different drivers. Try to find out who the original owner or driver was and ask this person about maintenance issues.

Mechanic's Okay

Just as with any used car, you need your mechanic to look at the car and give you a report on its condition.

Discount

You need to know what kind of discount you will be getting on the car. The problem is that it can be tricky to really assess what the car is worth. Some people subtract 15 cents for each mile on the car as they do in the leasing business, while others look the car up on the Kelley Blue Book site to come up with a value. Use all the facts on hand to make your determination.

When to Walk Away from the Deal

No deal is good enough to make you buy a substandard car. Consider the following issues and then walk away from the deal:

No Maintenance Records

If you cannot ascertain how the car was maintained, the deal will never be worthwhile unless the dealer will give you the car for free. It is not always easy to spot a poorly maintained car.

Price Not Low Enough

Some dealers try to sell their program cars as if they were standard used cars. You want a deep discount even to consider one of these cars. Otherwise, you might as well buy a new car or buy a used car from a private owner.

Reselling Soon

If you plan to drive the car for a few years and then sell it, a program car is not for you. These cars provide the best value if you plan to drive the car until it will not run anymore.

The Resources

The following Websites offer more information about the specifics of buying demo, fleet, company or repossessed vehicles:

www.safecarguide.com/gui/new/usedcars.htm

This Website offers excellent advice about buying used cars and high-mileage cars.

www.leaseguide.com/articles/carauctions.htm

Leaseguide.com includes a variety of sites to find car auctions that routinely sell fleet, rental or company cars.

www.beatthecarsalesman.com/mailbag18.html

This Website offers insight into why dealers offer deep discounts on their demonstrator cars.

www.is-it-a-lemon.com/vehicle_history/faq-fleet.htm

Look at this Website for information about companies that check used car histories.

27

What Should I Look for When Test Driving a Used Car?

Taking a test drive is more than driving the used car around the block. The process of taking the test drive and inspecting the vehicle is one of the most important parts of the buying process. While you absolutely need to have your mechanic inspect the vehicle thoroughly and obtain the car's history, you are the one who will be driving the car day in and day out.

The Challenge

Most people do not understand how to take a used car on a test drive. They drive the car around the seller's neighborhood for a few minutes without really putting the car through its paces.

A better approach is to inspect the car first and then take the car for a rigorous test drive in a variety of areas and at different speeds. How the car reacts on the test drive will help you ascertain any problems with the car, and discovering those problems can help you get an even better deal.

The Facts

Before you test drive the car, see Chapter 24 *Why Buy a Used Car from a Private Seller?* on buying a used car from a private owner for the list of questions to ask the seller. Then inspect the car's exterior, interior and engine. Use the chart on the next page to help you look at every significant feature:

System	Question	Yes	No
Outside of Car			
Alignment	Does each body part fit snugly?		
	Is the car sitting evenly on the pavement? Uneven trim or molding could mean that the car was in an accident.		
	Open doors and trunk. Is the space around each opening even? Again, uneven spaces could mean that the car was in an accident.		

Paint	Check the wheel wells, the trunk and the headlights for rust. Do you see much rust?		
	Is the paint a little faded, chipped or scratched? Deep scrapes or scratches could be expensive to repair, so look carefully to see how deep the damages go.		
	Does the paint match on all the doors and fenders? A new paint job could mean that the car was in an accident.		
Windshield & windows	Are there pits or holes in the glass on any window? Replacing the windshield or a window can be very expensive.		
	Do all the windows work? If the window does not go up and down properly, there may be something wrong with the door.		
Mirrors	Are the outside mirrors pitted or cracked?		
	Can the outside mirrors be adjusted?		
	Are the mirrors solidly attached to the car?		
	Is there rust around the outside mirrors?		
Doors	Do the doors open and shut smoothly? If the doors do not seem to work correctly or one door does not work as well as the others, that door may have been replaced because of an accident.		
Lights	Do the headlights, taillights, turn signal lights or brake lights have scratches or cracks? Do they work?		
Tires	Are the tires worn evenly? Uneven wear could indicate that the tires are not in balance or that the shock absorbers (or struts) need to be replaced.		
	Do the tires still have plenty of tread on them?		
	Are nails, screws or glass embedded in the tires?		
Inside of Car			
Seats and seatbelts	Do the front seats adjust easily to different positions? Do the seats tilt properly?		
	Do all the seatbelts work? Be sure to check the ones in the back seat too.		
	Do the seats have covers? Check under the covers and look at the material. Is the upholstery worn?		
	Does the driver's seat feel comfortable to you?		
Fit	Can you easily touch all the items on the control panel?		
	Do you have enough leg and head room in the driver's seat?		
	Can you reach the pedals?		
Roof	Are there tears or scratches in the material on the roof?		
Instrument panel	Does the radio/cassette/CD player work?		
	Does the airconditioner work?		
	Does the heating system work?		
	Can the vents be adjusted?		

Lights	Do the hood latch and gas latch work?		
	Do all the gauges work properly?		
	Do the inside lights work?		
	Does the dome light go on when you open the car's doors?		
	Does the headlight control work properly? Can you dim the headlights? Can you turn on the brights?		
	Do fog lights or interior/vanity lights work?		
Trunk	Does the car have a spare tire? Is the tire in good condition? Does the car have a jack and a tire iron?		
	Does the trunk smell of mildew?		
	Is there rust in the trunk or under the liner near the spare tire?		
Engine			
Idle	Does the engine ping or knock when it idles? The engine should idle smoothly.		
Battery	Are the battery cables coated with white powder? This means they are corroded, and you will need to replace the battery.		
Under the hood	When the engine is cool, look under the hood. Do you see wet spots on the engine?		
	Are the hoses, belts or cables worn, cracked or broken?		
Liquids	Check the oil level. The level should be full or a little below full.		
	Is the oil brownish? Thick or black oil could be dirty. Whitish oil could mean water has gotten into the engine or the engine block is cracked.		
	Smell the oil dipstick. Do you smell something burning? Oil should never smell burnt.		
	Check the transmission fluid. Is it pink or light red? Brown fluid means that there is a problem with the transmission. The fluid should not smell as if anything is burning.		
Fluid leaks	Look under the back and front of the car. Do you see puddles?		
Exhaust	Start the car. Then check the exhaust pipe. Is the smoke white? This is normal. Gray or black smoke could indicate that the engine has not been tuned up recently. Bluish smoke can mean that the engine is burning oil.		
Sounds	Listen to the car as it is running. Does it knock? Is it loud? Loud engines can mean serious problems.		
Sights	When you start the car, do any warning lights go on?		

The Solutions

The Test Drive

Now that you have looked over the car thoroughly, you can begin the test drive. Follow the steps on the following page to check every system:

1. Turn off any fans or radios. You want to be able to hear the engine clearly.
2. Expect to spend 20 to 30 minutes on the test drive. Otherwise, you will not be able to really know how the car works.
3. Drive on all the various surfaces that you will face if you own the car. Drive up and down hills. Go in and out of parking spaces. Take the car on the freeway and see how well it passes other cars. Take it into stop-and-go traffic.
4. Make sure to pay particular attention to the car's steering. You should be able to turn the wheel only an inch or so before it moves in the proper direction.
5. Drive the car over railroad tracks or other rough terrain and listen for rattles.
6. Make sure that you take enough time on the test drive to accelerate the car and then decelerate. Does it pull to one side or the other?
7. Is the car sluggish or does it brake properly?
8. Check the car's alignment by driving 15 miles an hour. Take your hands off the steering wheel for a second. Does the car pull to one side or the other?
9. At the end of the test drive, check the transmission. Stop the car and put it into park. Then shift again into drive. Moving between gears should feel seamless.

The Resources

The following Websites offer more information about how to inspect a used car and do a rigorous test drive:

www.cars.com

This Website includes information about test drives and inspections on used and new cars.

www.autotrader.com

Use this Website for further tips on inspecting a used vehicle.

www.mynrma.com.au/easy_guides_taking_test_drive.asp

This Australian Website gives excellent information about taking a test drive.

www.carmarket.com/testdrive.cfm

This Website from Car Market.com gives good test drive advice and also provides tips on how to keep the sales staff quiet while on your test drive.

28

How Should I Negotiate with a Private Seller?

Most people do not like negotiating at the dealership, but they do not mind bargaining with people at a garage sale or when buying a car from a private seller. The difference is that the private seller and the garage-sale proprietor are regular people who are trying to sell possessions they do not need anymore. In most cases, these people do not make their living by selling cars or other high-ticket items to consumers and so the stakes are not quite as high.

Since the private seller is just a regular person, most consumers do not mind negotiating at least a little on the price of the car. In fact, some people find it fun to talk down prices at a garage sale. Still others delight in giving as good as they get in a tough negotiation. Even though the atmosphere is generally friendlier with a private seller as compared to a dealership, you still want to make sure you have your wits about you when you negotiate.

The Challenge

The problem that generally arises when negotiating with a private owner is that you do not know how much experience the seller has. Some people do not negotiate well or do not realize that there is some give-and-take in the process.

The best way to begin is to chat up the seller. See Chapter 24 *Why Buy a Used Car from a Private Seller?* for the list of questions to ask a private seller. Then double-check if the seller is firm on the price. The price is probably listed on the car or in the advertisement the owner placed.

The answer to this question will help you to know if the seller has experience in negotiating and will obviously tell you the seller intends on holding firmly to his or her asking price. If the seller says, Make me an offer, you know that the seller is not expecting to get the asking price for the car. You can immediately make your first offer and wait for the counteroffer.

The Facts

Compare Apples to Apples

The most important point about negotiating with a private owner is making sure that you are comparing apples to apples when you think about the different cars that you might buy. Use the chart below to help you keep all the important facts in front of you when you negotiate:

Comparing Used Cars from Private Owners			
General Information	Car 1	Car 2	Car 3
Make and model of car:			
Seats how many passengers?			
Amount of trunk space?			
Amount of cargo space?			
Mileage of car?			
Age of car?			
Miscellaneous option			
Miscellaneous option			
Miscellaneous option			
Maintenance records for car?			
Proof of oil changes, etc.			
Price: [total asking price of car]			
minus			
Cost to repair:			
Mechanic recommendations to fix:			
A.			
B.			
Cost for new paint?			
Cost for new tires?			
Cost to fix rust spots?			
Insurance costs:			
Gas costs:			
Parking costs:			
Equals			
True cost to own car			

The Solutions

How to Negotiate Like a Pro

Some people do not like to negotiate. They want to pay what is being asked. They feel that someone has to win and someone has to lose in negotiations. You can negotiate a good deal and still be able to sleep at night if you follow the tips below:

Know Your Budget

Before you begin negotiations, know exactly how much you have to spend and how high you will go. Even if the owner tells you that someone else is coming to buy the car in 5 minutes, do not exceed your budget. Remember just because someone is not a dealer does not mean that they will not use any hard selling techniques.

Use Your Mechanic's Report

Get a written report from your mechanic to explain what is wrong with the car. As noted in the comparison chart above, ask the mechanic to estimate how much it would cost to fix the various problems. You can use this information to help you negotiate a better price with the owner.

Start Low

Start low but not low enough to make the owner laugh. If the price says OBO, Or Best Offer, feel free to start at least $100 less than you were planning. For example, the price of the car may be $1,600 or best offer. You might start by offering $1,000 if the car is in good shape and if your top price is going to be $1,500. The owner will probably counteroffer $1,500.

Inch Up Slowly

One common mistake in negotiating is that people move up too quickly. Make sure that you move up slowly. If you are new to negotiating and nervous about the process, move up in $50 increments. If you are more comfortable with the process, move up in $100 increments.

So, going back to our example, the owner counteroffered $1,500, and $1,500 is your top price. You can just say okay now, or you can see if the owner will go lower. You might counteroffer $1,100. The owner will probably counter with $1,400. You might counter with $1,200.

At this point, you both may stop and talk for a minute. The owner may say something on the order: I need $1,400 for a down payment on my new car. And you may respond with something like: I really like the car, but my mechanic said that it will cost me $400 to get 'xy & z' fixed. How about we split the difference and go for $1,300? The owner will probably agree, and you will shake hands.

Notice that in this scenario both of you leave with good feelings. You are happy because you paid $200 less than your top price for the car. The owner is happy because he thought he would probably have to settle for $1,100 or less for the car.

Pay Cash

Some sellers will accept cashier's checks, but it will be simpler for you to pay cash. The owner will be much happier to get a stack of $20 bills, and you will not have to go to the trouble of getting a special check at the bank. Most sellers will not accept a personal check or a credit card.

Try to Make It Win-Win

When you are negotiating with the dealership, they have most of the advantages in that they negotiate with consumers every day. Most people only negotiate once every 3 or 4 years for a new car. At the dealership, it is okay to leave without having made any friends. Be brutal and direct and get the price you want. The dealership will just get more money from the next guy.

However, when you are negotiating with a private owner, try to keep the bargaining to a win-win scenario. If you try to be cutthroat about the price, the owner may get angry and not sell the car to you at all. You usually do not have to take that strong a position. There is almost always a way for you to get the price you had in mind while also allowing the owner to make a profit.

The Resources

The following Websites offer more information on negotiating with private owners:

www.nadaguides.com

The National Automobile Dealers Association (NADA) offers a good guide about buying a car from a private owner and negotiating the price.

www.ftc.gov

The Federal Trade Commission (FTC) offers a PDF booklet called Buying a Used Car that explains everything you need to know to buy a car from a private owner. There is also a section on negotiation strategies.

www.cars.com

This Website features car ads from private owners and dealers and many ways to conduct searches.

www.kbb.com

At the Kelley Blue Book Website, you can search for the Blue Book price of any used car, noting low, medium and high prices, depending on the car.

www.carfax.com

Check out this Website to get a history report on the used car that you want to buy. You may be surprised to find out that the beautiful car you drove is actually a lemon that has been in three accidents.

29

What Do I Need to Know about Leasing a Car?

The Challenge

If you are considering buying a new car, you owe it to yourself to look at leasing a car instead of buying it. Leasing makes sense in the following situations:

- You do not drive your car for long distances.
- You use your car to entertain clients or for other business purposes.
- You want to be able to drive a new car every few years.
- You do not want to deal with the hassle of selling or trading in a car.
- You want to enjoy a car without dealing with repairs or maintenance.

Leasing is not for everyone. In general, if you can purchase your new car with cash, leasing does not make sense. Leasing is not a wise choice for people who want to own the car when the lease is up or for people who drive long distances during the year.

The Facts

Leasing Tips

According to the Federal Trade Commission (FTC), you should consider the following before you lease:

- Shop for your lease as if you were buying the car. Negotiate the price of the car and all the terms of the lease.
- Ask about extra charges for excessive mileage, wear and tear, early termination of the lease or any other factors that will cost you money at the end of the lease period.
- Make sure that the automaker's warranty covers the entire period of your lease.
- Look into gap insurance to cover the difference between what you still owe on your leased vehicle and what the car is worth.
- Before you sign the contract, ask the dealer to fill out the FTC form called Federal Consumer Leasing Act Disclosure available online at

www.ftc.gov/autos. This form clearly explains all the various costs involved in the lease agreement. If the dealer will not fill it out or tries to use another form from the dealership, do not sign the contract.

Leasing Lingo

Leasing contracts and language can be long and complicated. However, if you can keep the following terms in mind, you can make sense of all the paperwork:

- Closed-end lease is a type of lease agreement that allows you to return the car at the end of the lease period and walk away.
- Open-end lease is a type of lease agreement that makes you pay the leasing company the difference between the value of the car (as noted in your contract) and the appraised value at the end of the lease. The FTC advises consumers not to agree to open-end leases.
- Lease-inception fees are the costs you pay at the beginning of your lease period. These fees usually include a down payment (also called a capitalized cost reduction), a security deposit, an acquisition fee, the first month's lease payment, taxes and title fees.
- Capitalized cost is the price of the car for leasing purposes including taxes. Some leasing companies also add extra charges such as service contracts and registration fees to this amount. Ask to have every fee explained to you before you sign the lease.
- Capitalized cost reduction is also called a down payment. Leasing companies may ask you to make a down payment just as you would if you were buying a car.
- Mileage limitation is a standard clause in many leases. Most leasing companies will limit the number of miles you can drive every year to 10,000 or 15,000. If you drive more than your lease allows, you can expect to pay 10 to 25 cents per mile for any overage.
- Excess wear is a standard clause in many leases. If your leased vehicle has too much wear and tear on the interior, exterior or tires, you will be charged extra fees at the end of your lease. Most leases describe exactly what constitutes excess wear.
- Early termination is a clause often added to leases. This clause indicates how much money you will have to pay the leasing company if you decide to end your lease agreement early.
- End-of-lease fees are any monies that you have to pay the leasing company at the end of your lease. The FTC suggests that you get all these fees explained upfront in your lease agreement so that you will not be surprised later. These fees usually include excess mileage charges, excess wear charges and destination fees.

The Solutions

Fees and Other Matters to Be Negotiated

Leases can be complex, and most consumers do not understand their contracts. However, the good news is that almost every item in a lease can be negotiated including the following:

Beginning-of-Lease Costs

Savvy consumers understand that they can negotiate every aspect of their leasing contract including the first month's payment, security deposit or last month's payment, licenses, registration and title, capitalized cost reduction/down payment, processing fees, destination charges and (maybe) taxes.

Do not forget that you can also negotiate the agreed-upon value of the leased vehicle. This is the same as the price of a car if you were buying it. A lower value on the car can mean lower monthly payments for the length of your lease.

You can also negotiate the length of the lease itself and the monthly lease payments.

Middle-of-Lease Costs

Issues that will affect you in the middle of the lease are early termination fees and late payment fees. Whether you lease or buy, you will be responsible for insurance, maintenance, emissions or safety inspections and traffic tickets.

Negotiate the early termination fees and late payment fees before you sign the lease agreement. Ask for the leasing company to provide gap insurance that covers the gap between the cost of leasing the car and its actual value. If your car is totaled in an accident or stolen, you do not want to be responsible for anything more than the lease payments.

End-of-Lease Costs

In terms of the end of the lease, make sure you discuss and negotiate disposition fees, excess mileage fees, excess wear fees, excess mileage charges and the option to buy. Find out what you will pay if you want to buy your leased car when the lease period is up. All of this should be spelled out in your lease agreement.

Other Considerations

As with everything else about automobiles, leasing is a matter of choice. Depending on your lifestyle, income level and occupation, leasing could be the right choice for you. On the next page are the advantages and disadvantages of leasing:

Advantages of Leasing

- You get to drive a new car every few years.
- You do not have the hassle of selling your car or trading it in.
- Depending on your occupation, you may be able to get tax advantages from leasing rather than owning a business vehicle.
- In most cases, the manufacturer's warranty will cover the car during the lease period, so you would not be responsible for expensive repairs.
- Monthly lease payments are usually lower than monthly car loan payments.
- You can negotiate most of the terms of your lease agreement to your advantage.

Disadvantages of Leasing

- You do not own the car at the end of the lease period.
- You may be subject to mileage limits and have to pay extra fees if you go over the mileage limits.
- You may be subject to wear-and-tear limits and may have to pay extra fees if your car shows too much wear when you return the vehicle.
- You may have to pay end-of-lease charges even though you are returning the car.

The Resources

The following Websites offer more information about the specifics of leasing a car:

www.pueblo.gsa.gov/cic_text/cars/key2leas/default.htm

This publication from the Federal Reserve Board offers a consumer guide to leasing a vehicle including a comparison between buying a car and leasing a car.

www.ftc.gov/autos

This Website from the Federal Trade Commission offers information about automobiles in general and leasing in particular. You can download a PDF version of the publication called *Look Before You Lease* for details about leasing and a copy of the Federal Consumer Leasing Act Disclosure form.

www.nvla.org

This Website from the National Vehicle Leasing Association offers an FAQ about leasing. Definitely check this site out if you are uncertain about leasing.

www.nadaguides.com

The National Automotive Dealers Association (NADA) offers free consumer information about all aspects of buying a car. They also include guides to leasing a car with the best possible terms.

30

A New Car Lease
Is Negotiable?

If you have decided that leasing a car is the right choice for you, you are almost ready to negotiate on the lease package. But first, you need to do a little more homework. In dealing with a car dealership, knowledge is power.

The Challenge

Negotiation Phobia

Dealing with a dealership during negotiations can be intimidating. Some consumers are concerned that the sales person will laugh at or yell at them. If you are one of those people who really hate to negotiate, let your fingers do the walking on the Internet before you visit a showroom.

You can go to online sites such as LeaseSource.com and swapalease.com to see what the best leasing deals are. If you like what you see, you can skip the in-person negotiations altogether by speaking with a dealer on the telephone.

In fact, many dealerships will discuss the figures over the phone and fax you the worksheet with all the prices written out so you can look at everything at your convenience. If the dealer does not offer to fax the information, simply ask her or him to do so. Then, you can get back to the dealer at your leisure.

Swapalease.com also offers the option of choosing to pick up part of someone else's lease. It is the largest lease marketplace online.

The Facts

Before you visit the dealership, you need to do some research so that you have all the information you need to make sure you get a great deal on your lease.

Know the Car and Its Features

Figure out the exact car that you want including all the features. Know everything about the car. You can do car research on Cars.com, Autotrader.com or Edmunds.com to help you learn the different features and options of the car you want. Having all this information protects you against a salesperson who tries to convince you to go with another make or model.

Know Dealer Invoice Price

You can go to the three Websites noted above or to the NADA guides Website to find out what the dealer paid for the car you want. The best way to negotiate is up from the invoice price, not down from the sticker price. The sticker price (the one stuck on the window of the car) almost always includes a significant profit margin for the dealer.

Know the Worth of Your Trade-In

You can go to the Websites below to find out what your car is worth for a trade-in. The listings usually include a low, average and high price because the price of the car depends greatly on the mileage and condition of the car.

Know Market Conditions

Some cars will be popular and the dealer will have more requests than autos. Other cars will not be selling well, and those cars will be available at a discount. The Websites listed below are a great source of information on resale value of cars as well. If you have a car that the dealer does not have enough to meet demand, he will be more likely to negotiate the price with you. Discounts are also offered on models that will be discontinued or changed by the manufacturer.

Understand Leasing Terms

Re-read the chapter that addresses leasing. Make sure that you understand the terms listed there just in case the dealer's staff tries to confuse you by using leasing jargon.

Fees and Other Matters to Be Negotiated

Once you understand how much you want to pay for your leased car, how much you can get for a trade-in and how leasing works, you need to then make sure to ask to negotiate all of the fees on the following chart. You may be more successful on some fees than others.

Fees you can probably negotiate:

- Price of car
- First month's payment
- Length of lease
- Gap insurance
- Disposition fees
- Mileage per year
- Excess wear fees
- Option to buy
- Excess mileage fees and per-mile charge
- Security deposit (also called last month's payment)
- Capitalized cost reduction (also called the down payment)

Fees that may not be negotiable:

- Processing fees
- Licenses, registration and title
- Early termination fees
- Destination charge
- Taxes
- Late payment fees

The Solutions

No matter what happens in the showroom, remember that the ultimate choice is yours. If all else fails, get up and leave.

Approaching the Sales Staff

In most dealerships, there is a system of ups for the sales team. This means that when you wander into the dealership, it will be one sales person's turn (You are up, Tim.) to talk to the next unscheduled customer. Instead of saying that you are only looking, tell the sales person that you want to lease a car today.

This will be a surprise since most people are afraid of the sales staff and mumble something unintelligible. This will also alert the sales person that you can add to his or her total on the leader board in the sales manager's office. The dealership keeps track of which members of the sales staff have sold cars, and perks and other benefits are given to the sales person who sells the most cars. Leases count in that total.

Make it clear what kind of car you want and what features. Announce what you will pay for the car and what you want for your trade-in. There is no reason to be coy. Sales people never are. Tell the sales person exactly what you want and what you will pay.

Sales Reactions

Expect the sales people to do everything from chuckle at your ridiculous price to getting annoyed or even angry with you. Expect them to doubt your numbers or the sources where you got them. No matter what the sales person says, you just repeat the following: "I am sorry to hear that (insert name of sales person here) because I wanted to lease a car today. I am ready to sign on the dotted line if I get the deal I want."

No matter how many times the sales person goes to the manager, repeat the same line. Sometimes, the sales person will bring in another sales person as a closer. This person may try to befriend you or browbeat you into accepting a higher price than you want to pay.

Repeat that response over and over again like a mantra. Sooner or later the sales person will get the idea that you mean what you say and make a deal with you.

If You Feel Intimidated or Angry

It helps to bring someone with you when you want to lease a car. This person can be your moral support if the sales staff starts playing games.

When you have had enough, repeat your response one last time, and get up to leave. Go out the door and back to your car. Chances are that the sales person will stop you before you get out the door or leave you a message at home. You can lease a car from that dealership or another one, but remember that the sales staff needs you much more than you need them.

If the Deal Is Not What You Planned

If the deal is not what you want, simply get up and walk away. Very few people ever actually do this, so the sales person will not expect it. Knowing that you can walk away can be your edge in the negotiations.

If you stay calm, repeat your sentences in a mild tone and stick to your guns, you will be able to negotiate the right deal for you. In addition, you will feel empowered the next time that you need to negotiate anything–even the lease to your next car.

The Resources

The following Websites offer more information about the specifics of negotiating a lease:

www.leasesource.com

This Website offers the best lease deals available nationally.

www.swapalease.com

If you want to take over a short-term lease, this is the site for you. You can also find new lease deals on this site.

www.cars.com

This Website has excellent research information about the current makes and models of cars along with Blue Book values.

www.autotrader.com

This Website includes listings of all the current models and their trim packages.

www.nadaguide.com

This Website provides information about buying or leasing a car.

www.edmunds.com

For an excellent listing of advice columns and research help for leasing, check out this Website.

31

How Can I Take an Extended Test Drive?

An excellent way to find out about the type of car you want to buy is to rent a variety of cars from car rental companies. Rental agencies stock newer cars, so you can try out a variety of makes and models to find out which ones you like.

The Challenge

Every year, carmakers add new models of cars and also add new features to update their old models. If you have been driving the same car for 5 years or more, you may be surprised by the dizzying array of new car makes and models to choose from.

By renting a few different models and trying them out for a day or over the weekend, you will gain valuable information. Driving the car around your neighborhood or on vacation will help you see how the car operates, how comfortable you and your family are in the car and how difficult it might be to drive that kind of vehicle in your city.

The Facts

Most car rental agencies (including both the national brands and the local ones) require the following when you rent a car:

- A valid driver's license;
- proof that you are 25 or older (some states require you to be 18 and some 21);
- proof that you have a good driving record (they check this); and
- a valid credit card in your name.

Some rental agencies will allow you to rent if you are underage or do not have a credit card, but they usually require a large down payment or extra fees in case you damage the car or get into an accident.

Understanding the Lingo

Rental car agencies use a number of specialized words and acronyms in their business. Before you rent a car, make sure you understand the following terms:

Term	Definition
Collision damage waiver (CDW)	Not all states allow companies to charge this fee. Despite the name it is not collision insurance. It is a promise by the car rental company to pay for any damages to your rental car. If you do not buy this coverage, you will be responsible for damages to the car.
	However, your car insurance or homeowner's policy may already cover you when you drive a rental car. Check your policy before you rent. Some credit card companies and associations also provide members with rental protection.
Personal accident insurance (PAI)	This coverage usually pays a part of any medical costs you incur in an accident and also pays a death benefit if you are killed in the rental car.
Personal effects coverage (PEC)	This extra coverage protects your luggage and other items that you are transporting in the rental car. Again, your homeowner's policy or car insurance may already provide this.
Loss damage waiver (LDW)	This extra coverage protects you and the car against natural disasters and theft. Be sure to check which natural disasters are covered.
Refundable charge	This is the amount that the rental car company will charge your credit card in case you damage their car. Ask how much they will charge against your card and when they will do it.
Airport surcharges	Some companies charge you extra to rent a car from their airport office. Check in advance to see how much this fee is.
Drop-off fees	If you want to drop off your car at a location other than the one where you picked it up, you may pay an extra fee.
Fuel charge	Some companies give you the car with a full tank and ask that you return it in the same condition. Other companies give you a half tank and want the car returned with the same amount of fuel. Make sure you refill the tank, otherwise the rental company will charge a large per-gallon fee to fill it.
Mileage fees	Some companies charge a per-mile fee while others give you a specific number of free miles and charge a fee if you exceed the free miles.
Taxes	Be sure to ask how much will be added to the daily or weekly rates for federal, state and local taxes.
Additional driver fees	The rental company may charge you additional if you list more than one driver.
Out-of-state charges	Some car companies charge an extra fee if you take their car into another state.
Equipment rental fees	Some rental companies offer ski racks, child safety seats and other additional features for their cars at an extra cost.

The Solutions

With the advent of the Internet, you can search for the specific car you want, the rate you want and the location you want right from your living room.

Choosing the Car You Want

First, decide how long you will need the car. Then determine what size car you need. Rental car companies do not share a classification system, but most of them divide cars based on the car's size and features. To view a chart that describes the sizes, features and classifications used by car rental companies, please view the chart *Rental Car Size and Features* found at *www.encouragementpress.com*.

Consider what options you want on your rental car. Do you need air conditioning or cruise control? Do you prefer four doors instead of two? Is a great sound system important to you?

Reserving the Car

Once you know what you want, check the Websites of the car rental companies in your town. Each major company has a general Website with information about every branch office in the country.

Check to see if the rental car company will guarantee a specific make or model for you to rent. If one company will not do this, you can always find another that will.

Look at the daily and weekly rates. Check to see if you will be charged a straight per-mile charge or can get a certain number of free miles. Some companies allow you unlimited mileage within a certain geographic area. Check any specials the company is offering and check the specific requirements of each special offer.

Some clubs, organizations and associations offer rental car discounts. See if you qualify. Some rental car companies also offer frequent flyer miles.

Are there any additional surcharges for your rental? Are you picking the car up at an airport or in a major city? Sometimes these locations can add an additional cost.

When you find the car and rate you want, you can reserve your car online or by telephone with your credit card.

Picking Up the Car

When you pick up your rental car, be sure to walk all around the car before you get in. You want to make sure that the car has no marks or dents. If you notice a scratch or dent, make sure that the rental car staff notes it on your contract. You do not want to be charged for damage that you did not cause.

Check over the rental contract carefully to make sure that you understand the daily rate, the mileage plan and any extra insurance coverage you may have purchased.

Unauthorized Drivers

Do not allow anyone to drive the rental car unless that person is included on the rental contract. If an unauthorized driver gets into an accident, your extra coverage or car insurance may not cover the automobile, the injuries or the damages.

Returning the Car

When you return the car, go over the vehicle with the rental car staff. Make sure that you understand all of the charges on your contract. Fill the gas tank to the same level as when you picked up the car.

The Resources

The following Websites offer more information about renting a car.

www.ag.state.mn.us/consumer/cars/CarHandbook

This Website from the State of Minnesota offers information about renting a car and other car-related matters.

www.ftc.gov

The Federal Trade Commission (FTC) has a PDF brochure called *Renting a Car* that explains the entire process in detail.

www.bbb.org/alerts/article.asp?ID=96

This Website from the Better Business Bureau explains everything you need to know about renting a car, including a complete listing of all the surcharges.

32

What Exactly Is a Lemon?

In American slang, a lemon is a product that does not operate as advertised. While the term can be used to describe anything that does not work correctly, it typically refers to automobiles. All the states and the District of Columbia have enacted lemon laws to protect consumers against unsafe or poorly manufactured automobiles.

The trick is to prove that your lemon has a manufacturing defect and is not just an isolated problem.

The Challenge

Car manufacturers come out with new models every year. Most of them are excellent cars with reasonable safety features and new technology to make driving easier. Unfortunately, some new cars are fraught with problems. The lemon laws were created specifically to protect consumers from these cars.

The Magnuson-Moss Warranty Act was also enacted to protect consumers. This is a federal law that protects consumers who buy any item that costs more than $25 and has a written warranty. Obviously, automobiles fall into this category.

The Uniform Commercial Code (UCC) also covers all 50 states and deals with contracts to sell products.

All three of these laws can protect consumers against problem cars, but the easiest one to use for most people is their respective state's lemon law. Make sure you check the lemon law for the state where you live or the state where you bought the car (if they are different).

The Facts

What Exactly Is a Lemon?

In most states, a car is considered a lemon if it has undergone a specific number of repairs that did not fix the problem or if it has been out of service for a certain number of days due to a repair issue. Some states have a particular description of the defects that cause the vehicle to be classified as a lemon. Generally speaking, the car has to have been in the shop for the same repair four times without successful repair of the problem or the car must be out of service for 30 days in the first year of ownership or the first 12,000 miles.

Refund or Replacement

Most states allow the owner of a lemon to get a refund or replacement vehicle.

Proof

The biggest challenge in dealing with a car that is a lemon is proving that the problem with your car is a manufacturer's defect. You can go a long way toward proving this fact if you keep meticulous records and document every repair on your vehicle.

Arbitration

One method for consumers to have their case decided is via arbitration. If you are unhappy with the outcome of your case, you can still go to court. The automaker, however, is required to abide by the ruling of the arbitrator.

In general, states either run the arbitration process themselves or they outsource it to another organization to run the process. Connecticut, Florida, Georgia, Hawaii, Maine, Massachusetts, New Hampshire, New Jersey, New York, Texas, Vermont and Washington all run their lemon law arbitrations through a state agency.

Other states allow their arbitration process to be run by the automaker, the Better Business Bureau or the National Automobile Dealers Association. Not too surprisingly, things go better for the consumers when the state or the Better Business Bureau runs the system.

The Solutions

Document, document, document.

If you want to win the arbitration or your case in court, you will need to keep excellent records to prove that your car has a defect from the manufacturer. Follow the six tips below to make sure you have the necessary repair and other records to prove your case:

1. Keep all the paperwork from when you originally bought the car. Retain copies of all the printed or online information about your car's make and model. Make certain you keep information from the carmaker about your

car's warranty and any statements about the car's performance, mileage or repair record.

2. Always follow the exact recommendations in your owner's manual for the upkeep of your car. Keep a complete record of every oil change, wiper change and any other maintenance, even if it seems mundane, that you do for your car.

3. When you need to take your car in for repair, compose a list of everything you are concerned about and date it. Give the list to the repair department and keep a copy for your records. This will prove that you have been taking your car for the same repair repeatedly. Sometimes, the mechanics or technicians may list different reasons that your car is acting up or indicate that the car is in for the first time for a particular repair. You want clear proof of how many times your car has been in the shop for he same problem.

4. Get a detailed list of what the technician looked at during each repair. Make sure that the repair ticket indicates when you brought the car in for repair and when you got the car back. You want to be able to prove how many days the car was out of commission while being repaired during the first year or the first 12,000 miles.

5. Keep copies of all your documentation in a file inside your house. Do not keep these important records in your car.

6. Continue to make your payments. If your car is found to be a lemon, you will be reimbursed for all of your payments, including the cost of an attorney.

How to Proceed

According to the Better Business Bureau, if you believe that your car is a lemon, you need to start with the dealership where you bought the car.

Dealership

Go to the service manager at the dealership. Explain your problem. See if the dealership can make the car work correctly. Keep a copy of every single repair and document what the service manager said to you about your car.

Automaker

If the dealer cannot or will not repair the problem with your car and refuses to give you back your money, go to the manufacturer directly. All car companies have customer service departments. Call the company and explain what has happened. Do not lose your temper but indicate that you consider the car to be a lemon. See if the car company will resolve the problem to your satisfaction. In most cases, the automaker has more to lose from a lawsuit than from returning your money.

Better Business Bureau

The Better Business Bureau sponsors a huge dispute settlement program that is typically free to consumers. Before hiring an attorney, see if the BBB can help you get your money back.

Attorney

If nothing else works, hire an attorney. Interview a few attorneys before you hire one. Make sure that your attorney has experience dealing with lemon law cases and does not intend to charge you for the initial consultation. If you have a legitimate lemon law case, the attorney's fees will be paid by the automaker.

The Resources

The following Websites offer more information about the specifics of lemon law legislation and lemon laws in your state:

www.autopedia.com/html/MfgSites.html

This Website from Autopedia includes the URLs for the Web pages of all the car manufacturers in the world. Check with the auto manufacturer and car dealer where you bought the car to see how they will handle your problem car.

www.nationallemonlawcenter.com/lemon-law-tips.htm

This Website from a for-profit company called The Lemon Law Center includes useful tips to help you negotiate the problems with your lemon car. The company lists the names of lawyers who specialize in lemon law cases in every state and the District of Columbia.

www.autopedia.com/html/HotLinks_Lemon2.html

This Website from Autopedia includes a summary of the lemon laws for all 50 states and the District of Columbia. Be sure to check the exact wording of your state's lemon law on this Website.

www.lemonlaw.bbb.org

The Better Business Bureau runs the largest dispute settlement program for resolving problems with auto warranties. The site also includes state-by-state lemon law information.

www.carfax.com

Carfax is one of the largest online for-profit auto searchers in the country. If you want to be sure that you are not about to buy a lemon, pay their fee to make sure that there have been no complaints about the make, model and year of the car you want to buy.

33

Is This Car a Disaster or Been In One?

Sadly, whenever an area of the United States suffers a natural disaster such as hurricanes, flash floods, snow storms, tornadoes or earthquakes, unscrupulous individuals try to unload the damaged automobiles on unwitting car buyers in other states. For this reason, both the Better Business Bureau (BBB) and the Federal Trade Commission (FTC) include a number of brochures and press releases explaining that consumers need to be wary about buying a used car that may have come from a disaster area. The best tips to protect you and your family are listed in this chapter.

The Challenge

Finding the right used car for your needs is difficult enough without also having to make sure that the car you buy has not been in a severe accident or a natural disaster. However, consumers need to be aware that cars from flood-damaged areas and other disaster areas are frequently issued new titles and transported across state lines and even across the country in order to fool consumers. Follow the tips below to protect yourself.

The Facts

Title Lingo

Different states issue slightly different titles for the cars registered in their state. However, the basic facts about each type of title is listed below:

Damage disclosure
This type of title lists any damage to the car and the state where the accident or disaster occurred.

Salvage
A salvage title means that an insurance company has taken possession of the car and listed it as a total loss. This means that the person who owned the car filed a claim on it. Salvaged cars are often sold at auction, rebuilt and retitled and transported to other states to be sold at auction or through private sellers.

Rebuilt

A rebuilt title indicates that the car was damaged and then rebuilt. The problem is that you do not know the extent of the damage, who did the work and if that repair shop was reputable.

Junk

This type of title means that the car did not run well enough to be driven on the highways in that state. State usually will not allow the car to be given another title in that state. However, these cars are often transported to other states and sold.

Will Your Car Insurance Cover You in Case of Disaster?

After a disaster strikes, many car owners are surprised to find that their car insurance policy does not cover some or all of the damage. In addition, many car owners do not know whether or not their car insurance will pay for a rental car while their damaged car is being repaired.

For this reason, the Better Business Bureau suggests that you take the following steps to make sure that you are covered in the event of a disaster:

Ask for Comprehensive Coverage

According to the Insurance Information Institute, comprehensive auto insurance usually covers damage to your vehicle not caused by a car accident. These policies usually cover damage from natural disasters such as hail, floods and storms.

Check Your Coverage Every Year

Make sure that you know exactly what your auto insurance covers and what it does not cover. Unless the policy specifically states the coverage, you cannot assume that you are covered. You may want to ask your insurance provider about coverage for rental cars while your primary vehicle is being repaired and the cost of roadside assistance coverage.

Know Your Deductible

Check your deductible amounts for every type of incident. Many insurance companies have different deductibles depending on the type of accident. Make sure that you understand exactly what you will have to pay for in the event of a natural disaster.

The Solutions

In order to avoid cars from disaster zones, you need to watch out for the following telltale signs of problems:

Too Good to be True Pricing

If the price of a car seems very low, you may be dealing with a car damaged in a natural disaster. In addition, those who try to sell these damaged vehicles are often confrontational and pushy. They want you to buy immediately and pay cash. If anything about the car seems too good to be true, you should walk away.

Ask to See the Title of the Used Car

Always ask to see the title of any used car you want to buy. The title lists where the car came from originally. If the car came from an area with a recent natural disaster, ask the seller if the car has been damaged.

Check the Gauges

If the car has been in a flood or hurricane, the gauges may have water in them or look steamed-up with condensation on the inside of the glass. In addition, check to make sure that the gauges are accurate.

Test All the Electrical Systems Two or More Times

Cars that have been under water can have, or may develop, shorts in the electrical system. For this reason, check the radio, heater, air-conditioning and lights two or more times to make sure that everything works correctly. Even systems that have been completely under water may work once in a while. Also check for a musty smell coming from the heating vents. If the air coming from the vents smells musty or muddy make sure to have the car checked thoroughly by your mechanic before completing the purchase.

Carefully Go Over the Trunk, Glove Box and Underneath the Seats

No matter how careful they have been, unscrupulous car sellers cannot hide the telltale signs of a car that has been in a natural disaster. Water-damaged cars can show traces of mud, rust or water lines even years after they have dried out. Look carefully at the trunk, the glove compartment and underneath the seats for signs of silt or rust. Check all nuts and bolts for signs of rust.

Check the Upholstery and Carpeting

Carpeting and upholstery are difficult to dry out after water damage to a car. For this reason, you should look carefully at the carpet and the upholstery in all used cars. If the seats are covered, check under the seat covers to see what the original upholstery looks like. Check the carpeting, as well. New carpeting that may have been added to disguise the car will not fit well and will look as if it is too big for the space. If a seller advertises an all-new interior ask why the interior needed to be replaced. This is a sure sign the car has been submerged

Sniff for Clues

Your nose is an excellent guide to finding cars with water damage. Even if they have been cleaned several times, cars that have been under water tend to smell musty. Smell the upholstery, the carpet and in the trunk to see if you can sniff out an unscrupulous car dealer.

Get a Car History Report

No matter what the title looks like, order a vehicle history report from Carfax or another such service. The report should tell you where the car is from and if it has ever been damaged.

Let Your Mechanic Look the Car Over Before You Buy

Before you buy any used car, schedule a time for your mechanic to look it over. Your mechanic has the tools to easily look under the car and check for unexpected rust or water damage.

Look Over the Engine Compartment and the Spare Tire

Check for a water line, mud or rust in the engine compartment and on the spare tire. These are two places that flooded cars often show wear or water damage.

Check the Dealership with the BBB

Go online at the Better Business Bureau to check out used car lots before you buy from them. The BBB keeps track of unscrupulous dealers and will warn you if complaints have been filed against the dealership you are considering.

The Resources

The following Websites, books and other resources offer more information about avoiding cars that have been damaged in a natural disaster:

www.wiserdrivers.com

This Website is a partnership between the Better Business Bureau and the Insurance Information Institute to help consumers better understand their car insurance and what it covers.

www.iii.org/individuals/auto/a/basic

This Website from the Insurance Information Institute explains everything you need to know about car insurance. Of especial interest is the section about filing claims after your car has been damaged in a natural disaster.

www.bbb.org/alerts/article.asp?ID=92

This one-page flyer from the Better Business Bureau explains exactly what to look for to make sure that a used car has not been damaged by water.

www.bbb.org/alerts/article.asp?ID=437

This Website from the Better Business Bureau explains how to protect yourself and your family in case of a natural disaster. The BBB lists everything you will need to weather a storm or other disaster.

34

What Is a Car Scam?

No matter who you are, someone may soon be trying to wrestle your hard-earned dollars from you in the form of a scam. Scams are not limited to the Internet or to those who are buying or selling a car. There are many types of scams out there; now with the cost of gasoline skyrocketing, there are even gas scams.

If you follow a few simple tips, you can be prepared for the current crop of scams and the scams of the future. By asking a few careful questions and doing some research, you will be able to recognize the danger signals of any kind of scam.

The Challenge

Who has time to keep track of all the scams out there? No one truly has that kind of time. With a few simple precautions, however, you will understand the red flags that signal a scam in the making. Check the chart below for scam tips from the Better Business Bureau:

The Danger Signals of a Scam	
Signal	**Danger**
A deal too good to be true	If the ad is offering a luxury car for much less than any dealer is selling them, it is probably a scam. There is no free lunch.
Vague answers	When you call about a too good to be true product or service, you get only vague answers to your questions. Another version of this is not to answer your questions at all. Instead, they pressure you to send them money or lose out on the deal of a lifetime.
Pressure or intimidation	If you call and all you get is high-pressure sales, you are almost certainly in the middle of a scam. They cannot take advantage of you if you take your time when making a decision.
Requests for money without a written agreement or contract	Never give checks, money orders or credit card numbers unless you have a written contract with the appropriate signatures.

Immediate requests for personal information	Never give private information such as your social security number or credit card number unless you have a written contract with the appropriate signatures.
A company name that appears similar to a recognizable brand name or company	Does the company logo seem awfully similar to a major brand-name company? If so, the outfit is almost certainly a scam. They prey on people who mistake them for the real company.
A company without a local address or telephone number	If the company lists only a Web address or a P.O. box, you may be about to be scammed. If they have a local address or telephone number, check those out. Some complex scams involve creating a fake phone tree complete with a receptionist taking your calls. When in doubt, check with your local Better Business Bureau.

Gas Scams

A common scam whenever gas prices top $2 per gallon is the gas-saving scam. Some scammers offer a gadget that promises to give your car better gas mileage through magnets, air filters or other miscellaneous new technology. Others sell you a gas additive that promises to stretch how many miles you can get to the tank. The FTC has investigated the claims of these products and found that they either do not work or the company's claims are willfully exaggerated.

An added danger is that using one of these devices or additives will void your car's warranty from the manufacturer. Before you try anything to improve your car's gas mileage, check with a mechanic that you trust to see if the product really works.

Other tips to improve your gas mileage include the following:

- Keep your engine tuned up.
- Keep your tires inflated at the proper level. Check your owner's manual for the proper inflation for your car.
- Make sure that you car's tires are properly aligned.
- Change oil and filters as recommended in your owner's manual.

The Facts

Some popular scams involve private owners who are trying to sell their cars. Check the chart on the following page for descriptions of the most common types of car selling scams.

Scams That Target Car Sellers	
Name	**Definition**
Certified check scam	In this scenario, a person poses as a buyer for your car. The buyer agrees to buy the car and shows up as planned with a certified check. Unfortunately, the check is for considerably more than the price of the car. The buyer will have some plausible reason for this, and request that the seller wire the extra money to another account. The seller takes the certified check to the bank which accepts it. The seller wires the extra money to the buyer and releases the title to the car. A week or so later, the bank realizes that the check is a fake. The seller is out both the vehicle and a great deal of extra money.
Escrow scams	Escrow services are often used by sellers to ensure that the buyer has the appropriate funds to buy high-ticket items such as cars, jewelry, etc. on the Internet. Unfortunately, some escrow services are frauds. They collect money from the buyer and the car from the seller. Then the money, the car and the escrow company all disappear.

Another popular type of scam involves those trying to buy a used car. Look at the chart below to identify the methods used to cheat car buyers.

Scams That Target Car Buyers	
Name	**Definition**
Katrina cars	Cars that have been flood-damaged in hurricanes have become common scams. Get a vehicle history, and check if the car came from a flood-ravaged state. In addition, you can check all the gauges on the dashboard and look for signs of water. Also, check the trunk, under the dashboard or in the glove box for water damage, mud or rust. Smell for telltale musty odors. As a final test, wiggle some wires under the dash. Flood-damaged wires are brittle when they dry. If the wire snaps, the car may have been underwater.
Title washing	In this scenario, an unscrupulous dealer or owner transfers a vehicle from one state to another in order to change the title in the new state. Some people try this within the same state but in different counties or cities. Get a complete vehicle history.
Odometer tampering	This is when the car dealer or owner turns back the odometer in order to represent the car as having fewer miles than it really has. Signs of this type of tampering are that the numbers on the odometer do not line up or the odometer does not work. Look for missing screws or loose pieces that indicate the odometer was taken apart. If you suspect a scam, check for dated stickers for oil changes with mileage numbers that do not agree with the odometer. Also, look to see if the owner has owned the car for just a month or less. This can indicate an unscrupulous dealer or seller. Get a complete car history.

VIN cloning	In this scam, a scammer takes the legal Vehicle Identification Number (VIN) from a scrapped luxury vehicle or someone else's luxury car. Then the scammer finds a car with a similar make and model and uses the legal VIN to sell the car to an unsuspecting buyer for a too good to be true price. Buyers think that they have gotten a bargain until the police explain that the car is stolen. This type of scam is geared toward middle-income buyers who are delighted to buy a luxury car for much less than the going rate.

The Solutions

It is a sad fact that when you are buying or selling a car, you need to watch very carefully for those who will try to trick you. Increasing your awareness of the myriad of scams that exist today will go a long way in keeping your money in your pocket. Remember, if it seems too good to be true, it is.

The Resources

The following Websites offer more information about protecting yourself from or reporting automobile scams:

www.bbb.org

When in doubt about a company, check with your local Better Business Bureau.

www.ftc.gov/ftc/consumer/home.html

The Federal Trade Commission's Bureau of Consumer Protection is one place to report auto scams.

www.naag.org

The National Association of Attorneys General offers a Website with a variety of information for consumers including specific instructions and procedures to follow if you are the victim of an auto scam. You can find the attorney general's Website for every state.

www.fbi.gov/cyberinvest/cyberhome.htm

The FBI's Cyber Crime division prosecutes those who scam over the Internet.

www.usdoj.gov/criminal/cybercrime/reporting.htm

The Department of Justice's Cyber Crime division also deals with those who scam over the Internet.

35

How Can I Get the Best Deal for My Trade-In?

For some people, trading in their car at a dealership makes the most sense. If this is true for you, remember that you do not have to trade-in your used car at the same dealership where you plan to buy your car.

The Challenge

Getting a fair trade-in for your car at a dealership is not difficult if you keep three points in mind:

- Car condition;
- local marketplace; and
- specific dealership.

Car Condition

The condition of your car includes how good the car looks, the overall condition of the vehicle including mileage and paint condition as well as your maintenance records. Even though you will be selling the car to a professional at the dealership, neatness counts. So, treat the car as if you were selling it to a private party and wash it. If you are short on time, pay to have your car detailed.

Car Cleaning Checklist	
Wash and wax car	A clean, shiny car will net a better price and indicates that you have taken good car of the vehicle.
Clean out back seats and trunk	Take out any trash, junk or belongings that are stuck in the back seat or trunk.
Clean out glove box and empty ashtrays	Empty and wash the ashtrays, glove box and any other compartments.
Take mats out and wash them	Wash the mats or purchase new ones. In fact, new mats are a good way to cover old, worn carpet.
Vacuum	Once the mats are out, vacuum the upholstery, the floors and even inside the glove box.

Clean all glass inside and out	Make sure that the mirrors are also clean.
Polish chrome	Anything you can do to make your car look new is money and time well spent.
Wipe off dashboard and other surfaces	Dusting is good, but you can improve the look on your dash by using a reconditioning product to clean the dash and bring it back to its original color.
Wipe down tires and scrub whitewalls	Hose off the tires and use a scrubbing pad to get the whitewalls clean.
Check all fuses and replace them	Make sure that all the components on your car work properly.
Clean upholstery and repair small holes if possible	Repair holes in the upholstery if they are small.
Check fluid levels	Check the levels on every fluid in the car and wipe off the battery cables. You do not need to clean the engine, but do wipe off any spills.
Do not repaint the car	Sellers often repaint used cars to hide damage from an accident. Dealers will be suspicious if you do this.

In addition to cleaning your car, put together a complete list of all your maintenance records. You can get a better price if you can show how well you maintained the vehicle.

Maintenance Log	
Recent emissions test information	If you live in an area with emissions testing, get a copy of your car's most recent passing grade and include it.
Repair records	Make a list of everything you have ever had done to the car and find the corresponding receipt if possible.
Oil change records	Pull together all of your oil change records. If you do not have them, list how often you usually had the oil changed.
Owner's guide	If you have the original owner's guide for your car, you may impress the dealer. However, you can probably download a new one from the carmaker's Website, order one from the carmaker or find one on eBay.
Warranty info on car, battery and tires	Include all of your warranty information about the car, the battery and the tires.
Vehicle history	Get a vehicle history report from carfax.com or another agency and make copies for the dealer to see. This shows that you have nothing to hide.

The Facts

Local Marketplace

After you have made sure that you car is in the best shape possible, you need to consider your local marketplace. For example, if SUVs are popular in your part of the country and you own an SUV, you can expect to get a good trade-in value for it, but not if you are trying to trade-in a sedan.

While you cannot control the local marketplace, you can learn what cars are selling for in the local area. This will give you some sense about what you can expect for your trade-in.

Blue Book Price

Use one of the Websites listed at the end of this chapter or at the end of the book to check the value of your car. You will get a wide range of prices.

Be honest to yourself about the condition of your car. Do not forget to consider any additional work you have put into your car or after-market products you have bought such as a new stereo, fancy wheels or a moon roof.

Market Price

Using the same Websites and the online version of your local paper's classified ads, check the prices for cars like yours. Make sure to compare similarly equipped cars.

Your Trade-In

Depending on the condition of your car, the price you get for your car will be less than similar cars are selling for on the Internet and slightly more than the blue book value. Think about the very least you will accept as a trade-in for the car. Then figure out the most you think you can get for your car. The space between these two numbers is your negotiation room.

The Solutions

Dealerships

Car-Specific Dealers

The last thing you should consider is which dealership to approach. In large cities, dealers can easily trade or sell your car to other dealers in the city. In this scenario, selling a sedan when everyone else wants a SUV may not be a problem.

However, the experts advise you to take your car to the dealer who sells your type of car. For example, if you want to buy a new Toyota and trade-in your 2000 Honda Civic, take your car to the local Honda dealership to sell it. In this case, you are selling your used car to the dealer but not buying a new car, so it is technically not a trade-in.

The Honda dealer almost certainly sells used Hondas, so the dealership is probably looking for used vehicles to sell. You will get the best price from someone who will turn around and immediately re-sell your car.

Keeping the Trade-In and New Car Price Separate

If you are trading in the same type of car as the one you want to purchase, you need to keep the trade-in and the new car price separate. Negotiate the price of the new car first and then negotiate the trade-in. If you start with the trade-in, the sales person may try to confuse you by explaining how much you are making on your trade-in and how you cannot get both a good trade-in and a good price on the new car.

If you negotiate a good price on the new car, then the trade-in should just lower the cost. Some states allow you to pay sales tax minus your trade-in value. For example, if you buy a car for $25,000 and your trade-in is $5,000, you would pay sales tax on only $20,000.

Check with your state's Department of Motor Vehicles (DMV) to see how your state applies taxes on vehicles.

Negotiating the Trade-In Price

You already know the lowest price you will accept for your car so see what the dealer offers you. As in negotiating a private sale, the person who mentions price first is in a one-down position. Let the dealer speak first. You can always make a counter-offer if the dealer's price is too low.

Transferring the Title

Make sure that you have your title with you so that you can transfer it over to the dealer. Check on your local DMV's Website to see what you need to do in your state to transfer ownership. In most states, you need to sign the back of the title.

The Resources

These Websites offer information about trading in your used car at a dealership:

www.cars.com

This Website has excellent research information about the current makes and models of cars along with blue book values.

www.autotrader.com

This Website includes listings of all the current models and their trim packages.

www.edmunds.com

This Website has an excellent listing of research help for pricing.

www.carfax.com

Go to this site to get a history report for your car.

36

What Do I Need to Do to Sell My Old Car?

Selling your old used car will take patience, elbow grease and time. The hope is that it will be worth it because you will get a better price for your used car on the open market than by trading it in at a dealership. If you are willing to do everything necessary to get your car ready, you can net $500 to $2,000 more than if you had traded in the car.

The Challenge

Getting the Car Ready for Sale

Before you put your car on the market, you need to clean it and gather a few important documents that potential buyers will want to see. Check the charts below to find out everything you need to do to make your car ready for prime time:

Car Cleaning Checklist	
Wash and wax car	A gleaming-clean, sparkling car nets a better offer. It indicates that you have taken good care of the vehicle. Apply the wax yourself or spring for the top-drawer application at the car wash.
Clean out back seats and trunk	Take out any trash, junk or belongings that are stuck in the back seat or trunk.
Clean out glove box and empty ashtrays	Wash the ashtrays after you have emptied them. Clean out and wash the glove box and any other compartments.
Take mats out and wash them	Wash the mats or purchase new ones. New mats are a good way to cover old, worn carpet.
Vacuum	When the mats are out, vacuum the upholstery, the floors and even inside the glove box.
Clean all glass inside and out	Make sure that the mirrors are also clean. You want a potential buyer to be able to see his or her reflection in the windows.
Polish chrome	Buy chrome polish and do it yourself. Anything you can do to make your car look new is money and time well spent.

Wipe off dashboard and other surfaces	Dusting is good, but you can improve the look on your dash by using a special car cleaner to recondition your dash and bring it closer to its original color.
Wipe down tires and scrub whitewalls	Hose off the tires and use a scrubbing pad to get the whitewalls clean.
Check all fuses and replace them	Make sure that all the components on your car work properly. Prospective buyers are going to check them.
Clean upholstery and repair small holes if possible	Repair holes in the upholstery if they are small. Consider seat covers if the upholstery is in bad shape. However, careful buyers will pull up the cover to see what is underneath.
Check fluid levels	Check the levels on every fluid in the car and wipe off the battery cables. You do not need to clean the engine, but do wipe off any recent spills.
Do not repaint the car	Sellers often repaint used cars to hide damage from an accident. Potential buyers will be leery if you do this.

Maintenance Log

One good way to impress potential buyers and get top dollar for your car is to create a complete maintenance log for your car including all of the following:

Maintenance Log	
Recent emissions test information	If you live in an area with emissions testing, get a copy of your car's most recent passing grade and include it.
Repair records	Make a list of everything you have ever had done to the car. If you have the receipt for it, so much the better. List everything that you can think of even if you do not have the receipt. A potential owner will want to know what has already been replaced.
Oil change records	Pull together all of your oil change records. These prove that you have taken meticulous care of the car. If you do not have them, list how often you usually had the oil changed.
Owner's guide	If you have the original owner's guide for your car, you will impress potential buyers. However, you may be able to download a new one from the carmaker's Website, order one from the carmaker or find one on eBay.
Warranty info on car, battery and tires	Include all of your warranty information about the car and all its parts.
Vehicle history	Get a vehicle history report from Carfax.com or another agency and make copies for potential buyers to see. This shows that you have nothing to hide.
Checkup with your mechanic	If you really want to wow potential buyers, get a checkup from your mechanic and ask to have anything wrong listed. Show this to potential buyers. They may still want their own mechanic to look at the car, but they will be impressed.

The Facts

Figuring the Sale Price

Figure the sale price for your car by finding out the retail price and what cars like yours have been selling for in the local area.

Blue Book Price

Use one of the Websites listed at the end of this chapter to check the value of your car. You will probably get a wide range of prices. Be honest about how your car rates. Also, consider any additional work you have put into your car or aftermarket products you have bought such as a new stereo, fancy wheels or a moonroof.

Market Price

Using the same Websites and the online version of your local paper's classified ads, check the prices for cars like yours. Make sure to compare your car to cars with similar extras.

Your Price

Depending on the condition of your car, your price should be higher than the Blue Book price but a little less than people have been asking in your local marketplace. Decide the absolute lowest price you will accept for the car. Contrast that with the most you think you can get for your car. Create a selling price in the middle that gives you a minimum of $500 to $1,000 to negotiate with potential buyers.

Writing and Placing the Ad

If you are comfortable with technology, your best bet is to place an ad on Cars.com or another online car-selling Website such as autotrader.com. The great part about an online ad is that you can include photos of your car.

Look at other ads on the Website and write your ad like theirs. Be honest, but also point out the details about your car. The basics include make, model, year and description. In most cases, your description will allow buyers to search the Website, so include the most important information first.

List your name, telephone number and your asking price. If you do not include a price, you will have to answer unnecessary phone calls just to give the price. Pre-qualify your buyers by listing the price upfront.

The Solutions

Talking to Potential Buyers

Once your ad is placed, make sure that you are available to answer questions and schedule appointments with buyers. Be polite, but do not negotiate over the telephone.

Showing Your Car, Test Drives and Visiting the Mechanic

Schedule appointments with potential buyers close to one another or in a group. If you schedule in groups, you will waste less time and you will always have someone to see your car in case one buyer cancels at the last minute.

Go with buyers on test drives and ask them to have their mechanic come over to see the car. You can also suggest that you visit the mechanic during the test drive.

Negotiating the Sale Price

In general, since the person who mentions price first is in a one-down position, you want to let the buyers bring up price. See what they offer. If their price is not enough, make a counteroffer. Do not drop down too low too fast.

Getting Paid and Transferring the Title

Experts advise that you accept cash, a cashier's check or a certified check only. Call the issuing bank to make sure that the check is not a forgery. Check with your local Department of Motor Vehicles to find out what you need to do in your state to transfer the title to the new owner.

The Resources

The following Websites offer more information about the selling your used car yourself:

www.cars.com

This Website has excellent research information about the current makes and models of cars along with Blue Book values.

www.nadaguide.com

This is also an excellent Website with information and guides about cars and their prices.

www.autotrader.com

Check this Website for listings of all the current models and their trim packages.

www.edmunds.com

This Website contains an excellent listing of advice columns and research help for pricing.

www.carfax.com

Go to carfax.com to order a car's history report.

Why Is Tire Maintenance So Important?

We depend on the tires on our cars, but most of us do not even understand how to read a tire pressure gauge. Tires that are inflated correctly can improve the handling of your car, increase mileage and last longer. Tires that are old, worn or underinflated can cause accidents and wear out sooner.

The Challenge

The problem is that tires naturally lose air pressure just from ordinary driving. In fact, a tire can lose approximately half of its pressure before it looks flat. For this reason, you need to check the pressure in your tires every month. If your tires are underinflated, they can rupture. You can also have a blowout if you try to carry more weight than your tires are designed to bear.

Fortunately, all the information about tire pressure is inside the doorjambs of your car. The information is also listed in your owner's manual.

The Facts

Anatomy of a Tire

Modern tires have six parts that go together to produce a modern safety device. According to the Rubber Manufacturers Association (RMA), tires are checked by X-ray, run on test wheels and road-tested to evaluate handling, mileage and traction performance. With proper maintenance, tires can last from 40,000 to 80,000 miles.

The Six Parts of a Tire*	
Tread	This is the part that most people recognize. The tread gives traction and cornering grip on the road.
Belts	The belts provide strength and stability to the tread.
Sidewall	This section protects the tire from road and curb damage.

Body Ply	This section gives flexibility and strength to the tire.
Bead	This part makes sure that the tire has an airtight fit on the wheel.
Innerliner	This part keeps air inside the tire from coming out.

*from the Rubber Manufacturers Association

How to Read a Tire

Every number, letter or symbol on your tire means something. The manufacturer has information on the tire as does the Department of Transportation (DOT). In the chart below, we translate what each code means:

Information on Passenger Vehicle Tires Provided by the NHTSA*	
(Outer ring of tire) **TIRE NAME P 215/65 R 15 89H M+S MANUFACTURER** **Treadwear 220 Traction A Temperature A**	
Tire name	Name of type of tire from manufacturer
P	P indicates that tire is for a passenger car.
215	Width in millimeters from sidewall edge to sidewall edge.
65	Aspect ratio of tire's height to width. If the number is 70 or lower, the sidewall is shorter to improve steering and handling on dry pavement.
R	R indicates that it is a radial tire. Radial tires have been the industry standard for over 20 years.
15	Rim diameter (also called wheel diameter) in inches.
89	Load Index is the two- or three-digit number of how much weight each tire can carry. This information is not required by law, so some manufacturers do not include it on the tire.
H	Speed rating is the speed at which the tire has been designed to be driven. This ranges from 99 miles per hour to 186 miles per hour. This information is also not required by law, so some manufacturers do not include it.
M+S or M/S	These markings mean mud and snow. The tire has some ability to function in mud and snow. Most radial tires have this marking.
Manufacturer	Brand name of tire manufacturer.
Treadwear 220	This number describes the rate at which the tire should wear out. A tire with a grade of 400 should last twice as long as a tire graded 200.
Traction A	This letter describes how well the tire will stop on wet pavement. A grade AA tire should allow you to stop on a wet road in a shorter distance than a grade C tire. Tires are rated AA, A, B and C.

Temperature A	This letter describes the tire's heat resistance. This grade is for a properly inflated tire. The highest rating is A, then B, with C as the lowest grade.

* The NHTSA is the National Highway Traffic Safety Administration, which is a part of the Department of Transportation.

DOT Information on Passenger Vehicle Tires Provided by the NHTSA*	
(Inner ring of tire) **DOT 45 3197 7659 Tread4Plus Max Load xx kg xx lbs Max Press xx psi**	
DOT	The initials DOT indicate that the tire meets all federal standards set out by the Department of Transportation.
45	Code for plant where the tire was made.
3197	Week and year that tire was made. This example indicates that the tire was made in the 31st week of 1997.
7569	Some manufacturers also add marketing codes. The company that made the tire will use these codes if the tires need to be recalled.
Tire ply composition and materials used	This information indicates how many layers of rubber-coated fabric are in the tire. More layers usually mean the tire can bear more weight. Manufacturers also indicate of what the tires are made.
Maximum load rating	This is how much weight the tire can bear in kilograms (kg) and pounds (lbs).
Maximum permissible inflation pressure	This is the highest amount of air pressure that you should put into your tire. It is indicated in pounds per square inch (psi).

* The NHTSA is the National Highway Traffic Safety Administration, which is a part of the Department of Transportation.

The Solutions

Tire Maintenance

AAA and the Rubber Manufacturers Association recommend that you use the word P.A.R.T. to remember the basics of proper care for your tires.

P=Pressure

> You need to check the tire pressure at least once a month because underinflated tires do not look different from correctly inflated tires. Unfortunately, underinflation can cause tire failure. It also causes tire stress, irregular wear on your tires, loss of control and accidents. You can more easily blow out a tire if it is underinflated.

> Tire pressure is indicated in pounds per square inch or psi. You can easily measure the pressure in your tires with a pressure gauge. Tire pressure should be checked when tires are cold. This does not mean that you have to wait for fall or winter to check them. A cold tire is one that has not been

driven on for at least 3 hours. Think of it as the resting rate of your tire. As you drive, the air in your tires begins to get warmer, and the air pressure inside the tire increases. You will not get an accurate reading from a warm tire, and you may overinflate or underinflate the pressure.

A=Alignment

Have your alignment checked routinely by your mechanic as indicated in your owner's manual. If you feel the car pulling in one direction when you let go of the wheel for a second, your tires are not aligned properly. You may also need your tires balanced when you are having them aligned. Tires that are out of balance can also cause your tires to wear unevenly.

R=Rotation

Rotate your tires as indicated in your owner's manual. In general, rotate them every 6,000 to 8,000 miles.

T=Tread

Check the tread on your tires every month. You are looking for uneven wear and any signs of damage. You can also use the penny test to see if your tread is wearing thin. Take a penny and put Abe Lincoln headfirst into the lowest tread you can find. If you can see the top of Abe's head, you need new tires.

The Resources

The following Websites offer more information about tire safety:

www.tiresafety.com

The Bridgestone/Firestone Website contains terrific information about tire rotation and inflation.

www.nhtsa.dot.org

The National Highway Traffic Safety Association has a Website full of information about vehicle and tire safety.

www.tiresafety.com/images/Mario_brochure.pdf

Download a safety booklet by racecar driver, Mario Andretti, from Bridgestone/Firestone Website.

www.rma.org/publications/consumer_tire_information/index.cfm?PublicationID=11173&CFID=10720470&CFTOKEN=57536550

The Rubber Manufacturers Association Website offers an excellent guide to keeping your tires in perfect condition.

www.michelinman.com/mastapp/servlet/Controller/site.care.MainPage

Check out the Michelin Website for interactive tips about checking tire pressure, changing a tire and rotating the tires.

Should I Donate, Trade It In or Sell It Myself?

38

If you are in the market for a new car or a new-to-you car, you need to consider what you will do with your current vehicle. There are generally three options for your old car. What you decide to do will have a great deal to do with your income, lifestyle and personality. Your choices typically are:

- Donating the car to charity;
- trading the car in at a dealership; or
- selling the car yourself.

This chapter will help you analyze the facts and decide which option will work best for you. Once you have made your decision, see Chapter 39 on donating your car, Chapter 35 on trading in your car for the best value or Chapter 36 on selling your car to a private buyer. These three chapters provide valuable information to help you succeed no matter which choice you make.

The Challenge

Your values, lifestyle and your financial circumstances will help determine the best way for you to handle getting rid of your used car.

Financial Circumstances

If you do not need the money from your old car to buy the new one, you might want to consider donating your car to charity. This option is also good if your car is old or not in good condition, since you will not get much of a trade-in for it. It also makes sense if you do not feel like doing all the work or you do not have the time to get it ready for sale on the open market or to a dealer. You could also find yourself in the position of having done all the work on your car to get it ready to sell and discover that no one is interested in buying it. Donating the vehicle to charity would also be the answer in that scenario.

Lifestyle

Do you have a fast-paced lifestyle? Do you work more than 40 hours a week? Do you have children? Are you married? If you spend long hours at work, you may not have time to sell your car. It takes time, energy and patience to sell a car. If you are otherwise occupied, you may not be successful. If you are able to commit a chunk of time to the process, you may want to try to sell your car on the Internet or via a classified ad. You also need to spend time to clean the car, place an ad and talk to many potential buyers as well as perform minor repairs to increase the car's value and get the car in shape.

You also need to consider if you have a place for buyers to look at your car. If you are worried about having strangers come to your house, you can ask potential buyers to meet you in a local parking lot. You will also need to go on test drives with potential buyers. You need to ask yourself if you feel comfortable doing this.

Personality

If you are a person who is patient and detail-oriented, you may feel confident that you could sell your car yourself. If you are a person who is a good negotiator and likes dealing with the public, you are also a good candidate for selling your car yourself.

If you tend to have a short fuse, hate answering the same questions over and over again and dislike dealing with strangers, you would probably prefer to trade-in your car instead of selling it. The advantage is that you will be negotiating with just one person instead of dozens.

The Facts

Questions to Ask Yourself

Once you have thought about your lifestyle, personality and financial situation, you may have a good sense of which option is right for you. By truly considering the following questions you will know almost certainly which route to take.

Question	Yes	No
1. Do you need to get rid of your old car quickly?		
2. Do you need the money from the sale of your old car to pay for the new car?		
3. Is your old car less than 7 years or older and in good condition with less than 50,000 miles?		
4. Do you have a high tolerance for repetitive tasks?		
5. Do you do well with paperwork and other tasks that require an attention to detail?		
6. Do you have time and interest to talk to strangers about your car?		
7. Do you have time to write and place an ad for your car?		
8. Do you feel confident negotiating issues involving money?		

9. Do you feel confident doing minor car repairs?		
10. Do you feel comfortable showing your car to strangers and going on test drives with them?		

Scoring

Questions 1 through 3

If you answered No to questions 1 through 3, you would probably feel more comfortable donating your used car to charity.

If you answered Yes to questions 1 through 3, you are a good candidate for selling the car yourself or trading it in. Check your answers to questions 4 through 10 to see which option seems to work best for you.

Questions 4 through 10

If you answered no to questions 4 through 10, you may feel more comfortable trading your car in at a dealership. Remember that you can sell your car to the dealership that deals with your type of used car and then use the money to buy a new car at another dealership. You do not have to trade-in the car at the same dealership where you plan to buy your next car.

If you answered yes to questions 4 through 10, you will probably do very well if you sell your car yourself. You can make more money on the car and you will have complete control of the process.

The Solutions

Donating, Trading In or Selling?

Look at the following charts to determine the advantages and disadvantages of donating your car, trading it in or selling it outright. Knowing what each choice will entail can help you to make the best decision for your situation.

Donating

If money is not a concern or your car is in bad condition, you may want to think about donating your car to your favorite charity. Look at the chart below to see the advantages and disadvantages:

Donating Your Car to Charity	
Advantages	**Disadvantages**
No cleaning or pricing research	Need to do research on charities.
Tax deduction	Must choose a charity.
No negotiating	Protect yourself against future liability if something happens to the car after donation such as accident, etc.
Charity takes old car away	Must research tax consequences and do tax paperwork.

Trading In

If you do not have the time or inclination to sell your car on the Internet or via a classified ad, you may find it easier to trade it in at a dealership.

Trading In Your Car to a Dealer	
Advantages	**Disadvantages**
Does not take much time to complete	Get lower price for vehicle.
No work placing ads or talking to people on the telephone	Must negotiate with dealer.
Get paid for the car quickly	Need to clean car to get best price.
	Must do research to know what trade-in is worth.

Selling Car to a Private Buyer

Lastly, if you can tolerate a little aggravation and have no trouble dealing with the public, you may decide to sell your car to a private buyer. This decision requires you to do much of the work, but you will almost always get more money for all of your hard work.

Selling Your Car Yourself	
Advantages	**Disadvantages**
Get more money for car	Must clean car thoroughly.
Have control of the process	Must do research to price car.
	Must place ad and pay for it.
	Must take phone calls from strangers.
	Must show car to potential buyers.
	Must negotiate with buyer.
	Must clear payment and transfer title.

The Resources

The following Websites offer more information about how to decide if donating, trading in or selling is the right option for you

www.cars.com

This Website has excellent research information about the current makes and models of cars along with Blue Book values. Their advice section is also an excellent resource.

www.autotrader.com

This Website includes listings of all the current models.

39

Is There a Benefit to Donating My Car?

For some people, selling their used car to an individual or trading it in on a new car at a dealership is too complicated and too time-consuming. If your used car is old, needs repairs or is not running, you may find it easier to donate your car to charity than to try to sell it or trade it in. You can even donate your old boat or trailer if you can find an organization that will accept them.

The Challenge

Donating your used car to charity is a worthwhile and noble goal. Unfortunately, when you give to a charity, you need to be careful that the charity is legal, has the appropriate IRS credentials and will make good use of your donation. You also need to have the worth of your used car verified before you are allowed to claim it on your taxes as a donation. Even if you have donated a vehicle in the past, make sure you read the IRS rules and regulations or consult an accountant as some of the rules for donating vehicles changed in 2005.

While it may seem as if donating your used car is as complicated as finding the right buyer for it, in reality, the process is actually quite simple.

The Facts

While donating a car to charity used to be unusual, the process is now common. In fact, donating a car to charity is so common that many non-charities ask for donated cars. For this reason, you need to verify the tax status of the charity before you try to donate the car.

In addition, after you verify the charity's tax status, you still need to ask a few questions before you donate your car. Since you want the charity to get as much money as possible from your donation, call or email the charity and ask the following questions:

- Are you a charity under IRS section 501(c)(3)?
- Do you work with a for-profit company to sell your donated cars? Which company?
- Does your charity have a per-car or per-month agreement with the company?
- Does your charity earn a percentage of the sale price of the donated car? What is the percentage?

For many people, donating a used car can be the largest charitable donation they ever make or at least the largest donation during a particular tax year. Be sure that your donation will actually go to help the charity of your choice and not line the pockets of a third-party for-profit corporation that your charity is working with.

If your charity accepts a per car fee from a third-party company that sells the donated cars, you may not be able to claim your donation as a tax-deductible contribution.

The Solutions

Donating Your Used Vehicle

You can donate your used motor vehicle (car, boat or plane) to the charity of your choice by working through the steps listed below:

Verify the Charity

In order to qualify your car donation for a tax deduction, you need to verify that the charity is listed as a section 501(c)(3) charitable organization with the IRS. If the charity is not listed under this tax code section, you will not be able to claim a tax deduction for your donation.

You can check IRS *Publication 78*, which is a cumulative list of tax-exempt organizations. This IRS list may be available at your local library, or you can search the online version at the IRS Website.

If you do not have access to the Internet or do not want to look online, another option is to ask the charity for a copy of its tax-exempt status determination letter. All tax-exempt charities have a letter from the IRS to verify their status. Most charities keep a copy to pass out to verify their status for donations.

Churches are not required to apply for tax-exempt status, but they are still considered tax-exempt. If you donate your car to a church, the donation will usually be considered deductible. Be forewarned however, that since churches do not apply for tax-exempt status, they are not listed on the IRS Website.

The amount you may deduct for a vehicle depends on what the charity does with the vehicle. If the charity sells the vehicle your deduction is limited to the gross proceeds from the sale. If the charity keeps the vehicle for its own use you may deduct only the fair market value. In both instances the charity must provide to you a written acknowledgement of your donation, including the estimated value, within 30 days of receipt of the vehicle. This acknowledgement must be attached to your annual tax filing in order for a deduction to be taken.

Deduct Only Fair Market Value

If the charity does not sell the vehicle and chooses to keep it for its own use, the IRS will only let you deduct the fair market value of your used car. This is considered the price that the car would sell for on the open market in its current condition. If your used car is old, needs major repairs or does not run, you cannot claim that the car is worth more than what you could sell it for.

Over $500, Fill Out IRS Form 8283

If you are claiming that your used car is worth $500 or more, you will need to fill out IRS *Form 8283* and file it with your tax return in order to get your deduction. You also need to prove that you donated your car to a valid charity.

Transfer the Title Over to the Charity

According to the Better Business Bureau, the best way to prove that you donated your car to a charity is to transfer the title of your used car into the charity's name. Make a copy of this transfer for your records. If you ever need to prove that you donated your car to a legitimate charity, you will need this documentation.

In addition, transferring the title over to the charity itself protects you from future liability. If your car is parked illegally, stolen or in an accident before it is sold, you will not be held responsible.

Over $5,000, Get an Appraisal

If you are claiming that your used car is worth $5,000 or more, you need to provide the IRS with a professional appraisal that indicates that amount. Make sure that the person who gives you this appraisal is considered an outside expert and not a friend or relative.

Ask the Charity How Much It Earns from Each Donation

Before you donate your car, make sure that you know exactly how the charity will benefit. Remember, you may not be able to claim a tax deduction if the charity gets only a per-car or per-month payment from a third-party company that sells the donated cars.

Take Pictures of Your Used Car

Be sure to take a variety of pictures of the vehicle before you actually give it to the charitable organization. You may need to verify the condition of your car in order to qualify for a tax deduction from the IRS. The Better Business Bureau suggests that you also find local classified ads or car guides that show the value for cars that are similar to yours.

The Resources

The following Websites offer more information about the specifics of donating vehicles to the charity of your choice:

www.bbb.org/alerts/article.asp?ID=498

The Better Business Bureau Website includes articles and tip sheets about donating your used car to charity.

www.give.org

This Website for the Better Business Bureau's Wise Giving Alliance keeps a list of all the legitimate charitable organizations. Check out this site to be sure that your charity qualifies with the IRS so that you can claim a tax deduction for your car donation.

www.irs.gov

The Internal Revenue Service Website lists all the legitimate charities that have section 501(c)(3) status. You can also print out a copy of this list (*Publication 78*) from the Website. IRS *Publication 561* entitled *Determining the Value of Donated Property* provides information to file with your tax return in order to claim your deduction is also available on the Website.

www.irs.gov/pub/irs-pdf/p4303.pdf

IRS *Publication 4303: A Donor's Guide to Vehicle Donations* provides guidelines for individuals who donate their cards

www.cartalk.com/content/features/vehicledonation/#howitworks

The Car Talk Website includes information about donating your used car to your local public radio station.

www.donatecarusa.com/index.php?promo=NADA

This Website (which is a member of the Better Business Bureau online reliability program) allows you to donate your used car to a number of charitable organizations. You can choose your charity from a large list or search the full list by state or category.

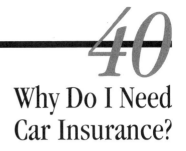

Why Do I Need Car Insurance?

Car insurance is an absolute necessity if you are going to own and drive a car. In many states, drivers are required by law to buy a certain amount of insurance. Whether your state requires it or not, you need to have car insurance to protect the car and to protect you, your family and any passengers you have in the car. If you are in an accident, the other drivers could sue you for a large sum of money. If you are not adequately covered by insurance, you could lose your car, your home and your savings.

In addition, you need car insurance to repair your car if you are in an accident or to repair the other driver's car in case the accident is your fault. Car insurance can also cover you if you are in a car accident and are unable to work.

The Challenge

Buying insurance is complicated because of all the factors that insurance companies take into consideration. Further complicating matters are the many different kinds of insurance available and outside factors that affect your ability to buy car insurance such as your credit history. Car insurance is based on six types of coverage. To give you a quote for auto insurance, companies quote prices separately for each coverage area and then add everything together.

In general, you can get a cheaper insurance premium if you ask for a high deductible for the insurance. However, make sure you pick an amount that you can easily pay if you have an accident.

The Facts

Insurance Terminology

Insurance representatives and brokers will use the following terms and you need to know what each one means:

cash value: This is amount you will be paid to replace your car minus any depreciation costs.

benefit: The reimbursement that the insurance company gives to you when you file a claim.

claim: Paperwork you file to prove to the insurance company that you were in an accident or something happened to your car that your policy covers.

deductible: Amount that you pay to the insurance company if you are in an accident. Essentially, this is the amount that is deducted from what the insurance company pays on your claim. As noted earlier, higher deductibles equal lower monthly premiums for your policy. The problem is that those higher deductibles will need to be paid before your insurance company will cover anything.

endorsements: Any change to your auto insurance policy. For example, you may add an endorsement to your policy when your teenager is old enough to drive.

exclusions: The items or situations that are not covered by your auto insurance policy. Be sure to read the list of exclusions before you buy the policy.

full coverage: This means that you have all the auto insurance that your particular state requires.

income loss coverage: Type of policy pays you in case you cannot work because of a car accident.

indemnity: Amount that the insurance company will pay for particular damage to your car or to you. Insurance companies use advanced numbers theory to average out how much they will pay for every kind of injury or accident.

limits: How much your insurance company will pay for damages. Insurance policies often have a lifetime limit or a limit per accident or per person.

How Much Coverage Do You Need?

As noted above, certain states require drivers to buy a specific amount of coverage. However, you may want to buy more insurance depending on how new your car is, how much of a deductible you want to pay and how much you own.

The Solutions

The Basics of Auto Insurance

As mentioned earlier, auto insurance covers the six basic areas. Some states require drivers to have all six types of coverage. Other states require drivers to have only one or two types of coverage. Most often the two types required are bodily injury and collision coverage. No matter what state you live in, you should get correct coverage for yourself and your family including your car and taking into account your overall net worth.

The Six Types of Coverage Include:

Bodily Injury Liability

This coverage pays for injuries that you cause to someone else in an auto accident. Most insurance policies also cover you when you are driving someone else's car or a rental car, as well. The Insurance Information Institute (III) advises consumers to buy more of this type of coverage than is required by law. If you are in an accident, the other driver may sue you for everything you have including your house, retirement accounts and savings. This type of coverage can protect your assets.

Medical Payments or Personal Injury Protection (PIP)

This coverage pays for any injuries to you or your family and any passengers in your car if you are in an accident. PIP coverage may apply to medical expenses, missed wages and even funeral costs.

Property Damage Liability

This coverage pays for damage to other people's property if you are in an accident. This can cover damage to other cars, buildings, yards, garages and even telephone poles and railings.

Collision

This type of coverage pays for repairs to your car if you have an accident. Collision insurance usually includes a deductible. This will pay for damages even if you are at fault in the accident. Some states do not require collision coverage, but your bank or credit union may require that you buy this coverage until the loan is paid off on your car.

Comprehensive

This coverage pays for problems caused by something other than an accident. For example, if your car is struck by lightning or has hail damage, this type of policy would cover the expenses. This policy also has a deductible. Some states do not require comprehensive coverage, but like collision insurance, your bank or credit union may require that you buy this coverage until the loan is paid off.

Uninsured and Underinsured Motorist Coverage

This coverage pays for medical and other expenses if you are in an accident with another driver who has no insurance or too little insurance. This policy also protects you from hit-and-run drivers. This coverage applies to you and your family if you are injured by a car while you are walking.

How To Choose an Insurance Company

Choose an insurance company based on its financial strength and excellent service. Do not make your choice solely based on price. You want an insurance company that will be around for a long time and will pay your benefits if you are in an accident.

Financial strength

No matter how familiar their name is, check even the big companies online. You can go to Standard & Poor's (*www.standardandpoors.com/ratings*), Moody's (*www.moodys.com*), Weiss Rating (*www.weissratings.com*)or AM Best (*www.ambest.com*) to check out the company's financial strength.

The Resources

The following Websites offer more information about the basics of car insurance:

www.iii.org/individuals/auto

The Insurance Information Institute has a huge array of information about all kinds of insurance. Their information on auto insurance covers is extremely comprehensive.

www.bbb.org/alerts/article.asp?ID=431

The Better Business Bureau Website includes a five-page alert about the basics of auto insurance.

www.nhtsa.gov

Go to the National Highway Traffic Safety Administration (NHTSA) Website to download a 26-page report comparing the insurance rates for all kinds of vehicles.

www.consumerfed.org

Go to the Website for the Consumer Federation of America to find out more information about auto insurance and the public good.

www.aaa.com

The American Automobile Association (usually known at AAA or triple A) offers information about insurance and automobiles.

www.naic.org

This Website from the National Association of Insurance Commissioners can help you if you ever have problems with your auto insurance. You can contact the insurance commissioner for your state and file a complaint. You can also check to see if potential insurance companies have any complaints filed against them.

Can I Save Money on Car Insurance?

Buying car insurance is complex and expensive. You want enough coverage to protect you and your property, but you do not want to pay for coverage that you are unlikely to use. Many states now require a certain amount of car insurance; be careful to buy at least what your state requires so you do not run afoul of the law.

The Challenge

While shopping for car insurance is not easy or fun, if you are willing to spend an hour or so online, you may find that you have saved yourself a fair amount of money by shopping around.

Use the tips below to save yourself time, money and hassle in your quest for quality car insurance at a reasonable price.

The Facts

How Are Auto Insurance Rates Calculated?

Insurance rates are confusing. Why does one family pay more to insure their minivan and SUV than their next-door neighbors? Insurance companies actually depend on statistics and actuarial tables to determine rates for each person. These tables take into consideration the following:

Insurance Classifications	
Indicator	**What It Means**
Where you live	Statistics show that there are more accidents in areas with more traffic and more people. For this reason, people who live in cities have higher auto insurance. Some of the lowest rates in the country are in rural areas.
Age	The age of the principal or occasional drivers also relate to the cost of the insurance. Drivers under 23 pay more than older drivers. People 50 to 55 years old pay less.

Gender	According to insurance companies, men and women drive differently. Young men are statistically more likely to be in more accidents and have more speeding violations than young women, so their coverage is more expensive.
Driving experience	Years of driving experience make a difference to insurance rates. Some companies offer lower rates to customers who take a defensive driving class.
Use of car	The cheapest rates are for people who only use their car for pleasure. If you drive to work or school, your insurance rates will be higher.
Driving record	According to the statistics, if you have been at fault for one or more accidents in the last 3 to 5 years, you are more likely to get into another accident. For this reason, people with poor driving records are charged more for insurance than people with few or no moving violations.
Car make and model	The age and model of your car can also affect your rate. High-end luxury cars can be expensive to repair. New cars cost more to replace if they are in an accident.
Income	If you buy an insurance policy that pays you if you are out of work because of an accident, your income will be taken into consideration on your policy. The more you make, the higher your insurance costs will be.

The Most Stolen Cars in America

The National Insurance Crime Bureau (NICB) keeps tabs on which cars are stolen the most in the United States, and they publish a list every year. Insurance companies take this information into consideration when they issue policies.

Top 10 Stolen Automobiles in the United States*			
Rating	Year	Make	Model
1	1995	Honda	Civic
2	1989	Toyota	Camry
3	1991	Honda	Accord
4	1994	Dodge	Caravan
5	1994	Chevrolet	Full-Size C/K 1500 Pickup
6	1997	Ford	F150 Series Pickup
7	2003	Dodge	Ram Pickup
8	1990	Acura	Integra
9	1988	Toyota	Pickup
10	1991	Nissan	Sentra

*Based on the National Insurance Crime Bureau (NICB) statistics from 2004. Data for 2005 is scheduled to be released in November 2006.

The Solutions

Top 10 Ways to Save Money on Auto Insurance

Most people find that shopping for insurance is complicated and time-consuming. However, if you follow these steps, you will save money.

1. Have a Clean Driving Record

The best way to save money on your insurance is to have a driving record without any accidents or moving violations such as speeding tickets. If your record has been clean for the last 3 to 5 years, you will qualify for the cheapest insurance rates.

2. Have a Good Credit Report

Every insurance company is different, but most check the credit scores of potential customers. Statistics show that customers who pay their bills on time over a long period of years are less likely to be in car accidents than those who pay their bills haphazardly.

3. Compare Costs Before You Buy a Car

Some cars are stolen more often than others. Insurance companies know these numbers, and they will charge you more if you buy a car that is often stolen. In addition, some new cars are expensive to repair. Before you buy the car, check online to see what the insurance rates will be.

4. Get Three Quotes

Experts advise insurance customers to go online and get three auto insurance quotes from sites such as InsureOne.com (*www.insureone.com*), Esurance (www.esurance.com) or Geico (*www.geico.com*). You can use any search engine to find additional sites. Compare coverage and look at the rates you are quoted.

5. Do Not Duplicate Health Insurance Coverage

Auto insurance usually includes medical coverage if you are in an accident. Check with your health insurance policy to make sure that the coverage is not just a duplication of your health benefits.

6. Check for Price on Higher Deductibles

A great way to save money is to assume more risk. You can save an average of 30 percent if you change your deductible from $500 to $1,000. However, you have to be able to pay easily the deductible or the savings will not really help you in the long run.

7. Ask About Low-Mileage Coverage

If you only drive your car on the weekends, you may qualify for big savings as a recreational driver. If you drive to work every day or to school, you cannot qualify.

8. Ask for Group Insurance Rates

Some insurance companies can give you a better rate if you belong to some particular group or club such as AAA, a fraternal order or even a buying club such as Costco or Sam's Club. Some buying clubs even have their own insurance products that they offer just to club members.

9. Think about Specialty Coverage for Towing or Car Rental

Consider adding some extra coverage that will save you time and money in the long run. For example, most companies charge just a dollar or two more a month to reimburse you for any towing charges or for renting a car when your car is being repaired.

10. Ask about anti-theft devices and other discounts

Insurance companies give discounts for everything from being a long-time customer to buying a car with extra airbags. Ask your insurance company if you can qualify for any discounts based on the following:

- Defensive driving course;
- older driver (50 to 55 years old);
- insuring more than one car;
- insuring both car and home with same company;
- anti-theft devices such as security system, vehicle immobilizer or car tracking system;
- safety devices such as anti-lock brakes, daytime running lights or airbags; or
- renewal discount (or long-term client discount).

An Extra Tip

You can also save money on your insurance if you remove coverage or lower your coverage limits for older cars.

The Resources

The following Websites offer information about how to save money on insurance:

www.naic.org

This Website from the National Association of Insurance Commissioners can help you if you ever have problems with your auto insurance. You can contact the insurance commissioner for your state and file a complaint. You can also check to see if potential insurance companies have any complaints filed against them.

www.consumerfed.org

Go to the Website for the Consumer Federation of America to find out more information about auto insurance and the public good.

What Is an
Insurance Scam?

Car insurance is expensive. This is partially because at least 10 percent (and maybe more) property and casualty claims are fraudulent. Many of these counterfeit claims involve car insurance. The type of scams are numerous and complicated, but most involve either creating an accident or lying about car repairs.

While few people feel sorry for giant, faceless corporations, you should feel sorry for yourself. The National Insurance Crime Bureau (NICB) estimates that insurance fraud costs the average American family approximately $300 a year in higher premiums. In fact, insurance fraud is the second most expensive white-collar crime in the United States. Only tax evasion costs more.

The Challenge

Insurance fraud is a big business and most people participate in it for the money. You need to protect yourself by being aware of the potential scams out there and by reporting any incident that causes you concern.

The Facts

Innocent Victims on the Highway

One major type of insurance fraud preys on innocent motorists in the city or on the highway. Scam artists are looking for people who will not make too much of a fuss, have newer cars and seem wealthier. Women and senior citizens are often targets. People with excellent car insurance are exactly what these thieves are looking for. They are particularly looking for new cars, rental cars and commercial vehicles.

Look at the chart below for a description of the most common staged accident scams.

Staged Accident Scams*	
Name	How it works
Swoop and squat	This scam uses two cars in the city. One car (called the squat) moves in front of the intended victim. The other car (called the swoop) gets in front of both cars and stops suddenly. The car in front of the victim hits the brakes and the victim's car rear-ends the squat car. The swoop car drives quickly way. The highway version of this maneuver requires another car to box the victim into one lane. Then the squat and scoop cars can do their thing.
	Since the car that caused the accident has disappeared, the innocent victim's car insurance will be charged for the repair claims and personal injury cases.
Side swipe	In this maneuver, the scammer needs only one car. The scammer finds a busy city intersection with two left turn lanes. With two lanes, some drivers automatically drift into the one to the right. The scammer chooses a victim with a nice new car and sideswipes it. The victim's insurance gets to pay for all the repairs and injuries.
Panic stop	In this scenario, the scammer usually drives an older car filled with passengers. The passengers are in on the scam. Someone in the back seat of the scammer's car keeps an eye on the intended victim. When the victim seems distracted by a child, the traffic or a cell phone call, the lookout alerts the scam driver. Then the driver hits the brakes, and the victim rear-ends the scammer. Again, the victim's insurance company will foot the bill for the repairs and injuries.
Drive down	In this staged accident, the scammer needs only one car and a busy merging lane. The scammer motions the intended victim to merge into the lane. Then the scammer runs into the victim's car. The scammer pretends no knowledge of motioning the victim into the lane and the victim's insurance company pays the bills.

*Information provided by the NICB.

Collision Repair Fraud

Another popular car insurance fraud involves body shops and collision repair facilities. See the chart below for a list of common scams.

Collision Repair Scams*	
Name	Definition
Airbag fraud	New airbags cost about $1,000 each. Scammers can buy stolen ones for as little as $150. Dishonest repair facilities will buy the stolen airbags and put them into your car and then charge your insurance for new ones. Stolen airbags are not safe and may not deploy in an accident.

Bandit tow trucks	A tow truck just happens to appear at an accident scene minutes after the collision. The operator offers to take the victim's car to a good body shop. Once the car is towed, the owner cannot leave until he or she produces a payment from the insurance company.
Burying the deductible	In this scenario, the collision repair facility works with the car owner to cheat the insurance company. One common way to do this is to list new parts or parts from the automaker on the estimate but repair the car with cheaper used parts.
Chop shops	Some body shops serve as the home of thieves who steal cars and disassemble them for their parts. The parts are then used by the scam body shop or sold to other dishonest repair facilities.
Inflated damage	Some body shops estimate costs for work that they never intend to do or parts that are not needed. A common trick is to say that the car was more damaged than it really was.
Kickbacks	A few scam body shops will even try to bribe insurance adjusters to say that the damage to a vehicle was worse than it was. Another common scheme is to bribe the adjusters to send innocent accident victims to the scam body shop.

*Information provided by the NICB.

The Solutions

Prevention is the Key

You can prevent car insurance fraud by reporting anything that seems suspicious to the NICB. You can report your concerns to their Website (listed at the end of this chapter) or to their hotline number: 1-800-TEL-NICB or 1-800-835-6422.

Read the chart below for ways to prevent auto insurance scams from happening to you.

How To Prevent Car Insurance Scams	
Type of Scam	**What To Do**
Staged accident	Do not tailgate. Leave plenty of room between your car and the car ahead. If the car in front of you suddenly stops, you will be able to stop, too. The sudden stop scam depends upon tailgaters.
	Call the police to all accidents no matter how minor. Get a police report along with the officer's name and badge number. If the police report says that the other car had a small dent, the scammers will not be able to ruin their car later and charge it to your insurance company.
	Add a disposable camera to your glove box. Make sure to take pictures of the damage to both cars and everyone in the other car. If you have pictures, the scammer cannot pretend their car was totaled.

	Pay no attention to people who run up after the accident and try to tell you what to do. These people are often part of the scam. They will try to send you to specific attorneys and doctors who are also part of the scam.
	Do not file a personal injury claim if you were not hurt. Report any doctor who insists that you file a false report.
	Report attorneys who tell you that their clients were hurt on your property if you have never seen the client before and have no prior notice of any accident.
Collision fraud	Use a collision repair facility that uses ASE-certified (National Institute for Automotive Service Excellence) technicians. Check with your insurance company or the Better Business Bureau for a list of reputable companies.
	Look at the shop before you agree to any work. Make sure that the place is clean and orderly. Check that the equipment is modern.
	Ask for a written damage report instead of an estimate. The damage report is a blueprint for the repair. This type of report also contains more details about what needs to be fixed.
	Get a written warranty for your collision repair parts or paintwork.

The Resources

The following Websites offer more information about protecting yourself from automobile insurance scams:

www.bbb.org

When in doubt about a company, check with your local Better Business Bureau or check their Website.

www.ftc.gov/ftc/consumer/home.html

The Federal Trade Commission's Bureau of Consumer Protection is one place to report auto insurance scams.

www.naag.org

The National Association of Attorneys General offers a Website with a variety of information for consumers including guidelines addressing what to do if you are the victim of an auto insurance scam. You can find the attorney general's Website for every state.

www.nicb.org

The NICB works to protect consumers from insurance fraud. If you suspect that you have been the victim of insurance fraud, call the NICB hotline at 1-800-TEL-NICB (1-800-835-6422). The call is free and can be anonymous. You can also lodge your complaint on the Website.

What Is the Right Car for the First-Time Driver?

People learn to drive at different times. Most people get their license during the first month they are eligible to drive at age 16. Others wait until they are adults. No matter when you learn to drive, your first vehicle should be steady and safe in order to protect you in an accident and provide maximum reliability on the road.

The Challenge

Car ads try to tempt us with sports cars, turbo-charging and high-performance vehicles that go fast and look good. Unfortunately, these cars are better for people with years of driving or life experience; they are all wrong for teen drivers and first-time car buyers.

The Facts

The first year or two of driving can be risky, especially for teen drivers. According to the National Highway Traffic Safety Administration (NHTSA), car accidents are the leading cause of death for young people aged 15 to 20. To try to reduce the number of fatalities, many states have instituted Graduated Drivers Licensing (GDL) programs that allow young adults to drive only at specific times and in specific circumstances based on their age.

According to a 2006 study from the Johns Hopkins Bloomberg School of Public Health, GDL programs can lower the crash rate for 16-year old drivers by approximately 11 percent. In fact, since GDL programs were implemented in various states, the 2004 death rates for people aged 16 to 20 has dropped to an all-time low–the lowest rate since the NHTSA started keeping records in 1975.

Creating Your Own Graduated Driver Licensing Program for Your Teen Driver

If your state does not have a GDL program for teenaged drivers, you can create one for your own teen by following the chart below:

Guidelines for Teen Drivers	
Restriction	**Reason**
Do not allow teen drivers to drive after 9 or 10 p.m. for first 6 months to 1-year.	According to the Insurance Institute for Highway Safety (IIHS), four out of 10 teenage crashes occur between 9:00 p.m. and 6:00 a.m. In fact, approximately two-thirds of all crashes that resulted in the death of a teenage happened before midnight.
Do not allow teen drivers to have more than one passenger in car for 6 months to 1-year.	Teens who are driving three or more other teens are three times as likely to get into a fatal crash than teens who are driving alone. Experts explain that teenage passengers are a major contributor to teen accidents. For 16-year old drivers, half of the crashes that result in teen death happen when the new driver has passengers in the car.
Do not allow teen drivers to talk on cell phone while driving.	Experts advise that using a cell phone while driving is a huge distraction and plays a role in car accidents.
Do not allow teen drivers to drive without a safety belt attached on every trip.	In 2004, 58 percent of those 16 to 20 who were killed in car crashes were not wearing a seat belt, according to the NHTSA. Seat belt use is significantly lower in teen drivers, especially males.
Remind teen drivers about the dangers of drinking and driving.	Although the number of new drivers age 15 to 20 who where legally drunk and in fatal crashes dropped by 6 percent from 1993 to 2003, young people do not always understand the dangers of drinking and driving.
Remind teen drivers about the dangers of driving when sleepy.	Contrary to popular belief, your body just shuts down when it needs to sleep. You do not get any warning. Even young people need a reasonable amount of sleep. Advise your young driver not to drive without enough sleep.

The Solutions

Choosing a Safe Car for Your First Vehicle

Follow these tips from the Insurance Information Institute for buying a safe first car for yourself or your teen:

Choose Cars with Good Crash Protection

Check the crash rating for vehicles that you are thinking about buying at the Insurance Institute for Highway Safety (IIHS) Website *www.iihs.org/ratings/default.aspx*. The IIHS tests each vehicle for front, side and rear crashworthiness.

Choose Cars that Are Mid-Size or Larger

You want to choose a car with excellent crash protection in the event of an accident. Few small cars offer enough protection. Experts advise you to choose a mid-size or full-size vehicle. However, a large car without safety devices does not necessarily offer better protection.

Choose Cars that Do Not Encourage Reckless Driving.

Choose cars with less flash and more substance. Those with high-performance features such as turbo-charging, red paint and flashy ad campaigns are sending the wrong signal to inexperienced drivers. Speeding is a major problem with teen drivers and contributes to accidents.

Choose Cars that Are Stable

Experts advise that SUVs have a higher center of gravity than cars, and this fact makes them unsuitable for new drivers. In particular, smaller or boxier SUVs tend to rollover if the driver makes a sudden turn.

Choose Newer Vehicles

Older cars may be bigger, but they lack the safety features such as airbags that make modern cars more able to withstand an accident. Look at cars no more than 6 to 10 years old. To find out which cars are the safest, go to the safercar.gov Website.

Choose an Automatic Transmission

Automatic transmissions are much easier to operate, especially for new drivers. Until your driver has been on the road for 2 years or more, stick with an automatic transmission. Shifting the car can be a major distraction from watching traffic and paying attention to the speed limit.

Safest Cars for 2006 According to the Insurance Institute for Highway Safety

2006 Top Safety Picks By Car Size			
Size Group	**Make/Model**	**Rating**	**What The Rating Means**
Large Cars			
	Ford 500 with optional side air bags	GOLD	The IIHS tests cars for crashworthiness from the front, side and rear. Cars that earn good ratings for crash protection at all three crash sites earn a gold rating.
	Mercury Montego with optional side air bags	GOLD	
	|Audi A6	SILVER	The IIHS tests cars for crashworthiness from the front, side and rear. Cars that earn good ratings for front and side collisions and acceptable ratings for rear crash protection earn a silver rating.
Minivan			
	Hyundai Entourage 2007 models	GOLD	The IIHS tests cars for crashworthiness from the front, side and rear. Cars that earn good ratings for crash protection at all three crash sites earn a gold rating.
	Kia Sedona	GOLD	

Midsize Car			
	Saab 9-3	GOLD	The IIHS tests cars for crashworthiness from the front, side and rear. Cars that earn good ratings for crash protection at all three crash sites earn a gold rating.
	Subaru Legacy	GOLD	
	Audi A3	SILVER	The IIHS tests cars for crashworthiness from the front, side and rear. Cars that earn good ratings for front and side collisions and acceptable ratings for rear crash protection earn a silver rating.
	Audi A4	SILVER	
	BMW 3 series (4-door models)	SILVER	
	Chevrolet Malibu with optional side airbags	SILVER	
	Lexus IS	SILVER	
	Volkswagen Jetta	SILVER	
	Volkswagen Rabbit (4-door models)	SILVER	
	Volkswagen Passat	SILVER	
Small Cars			
	Honda Civic 4-door models	GOLD	The IIHS tests cars for crashworthiness from the front, side and rear. Cars that earn good ratings for crash protection at all three crash sites earn a gold rating.
	Saab 9-2X	GOLD	
	Subaru Impreza except WRX models	GOLD	

The Resources

The following Websites offer more information about first-time and teen drivers:

www.iihs.org/ratings/default.aspx

Check out this Website for the safety ratings for almost any car you might choose. The Website also includes information about the types of accidents that each make and model of car has been involved in over the years.

www.nhtsa.dot.gov/ncap/Index.cfm

The Department of Transportation offers a Website called safercar.gov. At this site, you can compare the safety test ratings for a number of vehicles using an online tool. This is a good chance to find out which potential vehicles would be the safest for new drivers.

Reduced Insurance Premiums for the Teenaged Driver?

Having a teenaged driver in the house may not seem real until you have to buy and pay for the auto insurance. Auto insurance is quite expensive for new drivers, especially young drivers. Experts advise you to be prepared to pay approximately 50 percent more for your daughter's insurance and approximately 100 percent more for your son's insurance.

The Challenge

You can save money on your teenager's car insurance if you take the time to check which cars are the safest and the least performance-oriented. If you buy your teen a sports car or other high-performance vehicle, you will pay much more in insurance. On the other hand, if you purchase a car with all the latest safety equipment, you will protect both your child and your wallet.

The Facts

Before Going Car Shopping with Your Teen

Before you go to look at cars with your teen driver, call your insurance company. Ask which cars are considered the safest and which will have the lowest rates for teen drivers. If you start with the insurance company, you will know exactly what you should avoid when you begin looking at potential cars.

Safe Cars Cost Less to Insure	
Car Description	**Reason to Avoid this Vehicle**
SUVs	SUVs have a high incidence of rolling over in hard turns. Young drivers sometimes lack experience and try to make up for it with quick reflexes.
Trucks	Some trucks, especially the compact versions, tend to have rollover problems. Young drivers do not always have the experience to manage all the systems of the car as well as being careful in turns.

Small cars	Small cars do not offer enough protection for young drivers. Since young drivers are 10 times more likely to be in an accident than older drivers, you want to choose a vehicle with as many safety devices (including size) as possible.
Sports cars or high-performance cars	Cars that go fast are fine for older drivers with more experience. However, young drivers do not have the maturity to maintain proper driving speeds. They may be tempted to speed and show off if they have a high-performance vehicle.

Anti-Theft Tips for Teens

New drivers can be careless when it comes to locking doors and parking under streetlights. As a parent, make sure that you and your teen understand the four levels of protection that can keep your car from being stolen.

Four Levels of Protection from Auto Theft by the NICB*	
Level	**Description**
1- Common sense	Many cars are stolen because the driver leaves a door open. Make sure that your teenaged driver always removes the keys from the ignition, locks the doors, closes the windows and parks in a well-lit area no matter how long he or she will be gone. An experienced car thief only needs about 30 seconds to get into an unattended car.
2- Warning devices	Thieves do not like to deal with problems. If you give your car another layer of protection with audible or visible warning systems, would-be auto thieves will walk away. Alarm systems, steering column collars and locks, wheel locks, VIN etching and identification markers in and on the car will make it more difficult to steal.
3- Immobilizing devices	Stop thieves cold with a third layer of protection that keeps the bad guys from hot-wiring your car. Smart keys, kill switches and fuel pump disablers make it almost impossible for someone to steal your car.
4-Tracking devices	The final layer of protection is a tracking device in your car. With a tracking device, the police can often locate your car in hours rather than days if it is stolen.

*National Insurance Crime Bureau

The Solutions

Getting the Best Price

If you follow a few simple tips, you can get the best possible rate for your new driver. Most experts advise that you discuss the cost of car insurance with your teen. It can be very beneficial for new drivers to understand why insurance companies charge so much for teens. The actuarial tables alone may keep your teenaged driver from making foolish and dangerous mistakes.

Insure Teen on Your Policy

You can usually get the best price for teen car insurance if you include the teenager on your policy. You can ask your insurance agent or company about a separate policy, but these are usually twice as expensive as including the teen on your policy. If you have to buy a separate policy, make sure to get a discount for buying several policies from the same company. Consult with your agent, some insurance companies offer better new driver rates if your teen has their own car for this becomes the primary car she drives. Insurance rates for older model cars with a dedicated teen driver will cost less than adding your teen to your late model auto policy.

Buy a Safer Car

Buy a safe car such as a newer, mid-sized sedan. It may not seem trendy or sexy to your teen, but it will be safe and the insurance will be much cheaper.

Shop for Insurance Rates

Just as with your own insurance policy, check online and get at least three quotes. Adding your teen to your policy should be the cheapest option, but check out the possibility of a separate policy for your teen or changing your family policy to another carrier. Different insurance companies give different weights to the same circumstances. Shop around to be sure that you are getting the best rate.

Alert Insurance Company to College Years

If your child attends a college is at least 100 miles away and does not drive there, you can save a great deal on your insurance during the school year. In the summer, you will need to inform the company that your child will be driving your car again.

Talk to Teens about Keeping a Clean Driving Record

One of the best ways to save money on teen insurance is for the teen to have a spotless driving record. Talk to your teenager about helping to keep the cost of insurance down. In most cases, your teen will want to be treated like an adult, so talk about the costs as well as the responsibilities of driving.

Talk to Teens about Insurance Discounts for Good Grades

If your new driver can maintain a B average in school, many insurance companies will give you a discount on your teen's insurance. You might consider giving your teenager the money that you save on the insurance because of his or her good grades.

Consider Private Driver Education Classes

Some insurance companies give discounts if your child passed a driver education class. Check with your insurance carrier first. Not all insurance companies provide this discounts and you need to ask questions.

If the Worst Happens, Choose the Traffic School Option

If your child does get into an accident, make sure to send him or her to traffic school if this is an option. Going to traffic school can keep the moving violation or speeding ticket off your child's driving record. This could save you money on insurance.

Practice What You Preach

Talk to your teen about paying attention on the road, not yelling at other drivers and not arguing with people in the vehicle and then practice what you preach. Your teen will always learn more by watching what you do. For this reason, you need to always use your seat belts, watch traffic carefully and make sure you are a courteous driver. It goes without saying that you should never drink alcohol and drive.

Let Your Teen Drive with You In the Car

The best way to see how your teen is doing is to allow him or her to drive the car with you. Although your teen may be nervous at first, you need to monitor his or her driving. You can easily offer gentle advice and coaching if you drive frequently with your teen.

The Resources

The following Websites offer more information about getting the best price on insuring teenaged drivers:

www.nhtsa.dot.gov/ncap/Index.cfm

The Department of Transportation offers a Website called safercar.gov which has an online tool that allows you to compare the safety test ratings for a number of vehicles.

www.consumerfed.org

Go to the Website for the Consumer Federation of America to find out more information about auto insurance and the public good.

www.aaa.com

The American Automobile Association offers information about saving on car insurance and choosing automobiles that are easy to insure.

www.nicb.org

The Website for the National Insurance Crime Bureau (NICB) has listings of the cars most likely to be stolen in the U.S. These cars may cost more to insure. This site also has extensive information about keeping your teen's car from being stolen.

How Can I Keep My Car in Tip-Top Shape?

Many people lead such busy lives that they leave all of their car maintenance to the guy at the oil-change place or the mechanic. Although today's cars are complicated by technology, anyone can still do a great deal of routine maintenance in the home garage or in the driveway with a little preparation and interest. What is even better is that each of these checks takes 15 minutes or less.

The Challenge

Keeping up with scheduled maintenance can be difficult. It is much easier if the various chores are broken up into weekly, bi-weekly, monthly and bi-monthly checks. If you can fit these 5-to 15-minute checkups into your regular weekly schedule, you will find that maintaining your car yourself is easy and painless.

The Facts

Spending too Much for the Wrong Items

Some people think that they are taking good care of their cars by buying the best grade of gasoline and letting the dealership fix every little problem. While getting your car repaired is a good thing, you do not need to go to the dealership unless not going voids your warranty. Local independent repair shops can do just as good a job for less money. Look at the list below to make sure that you are not wasting money.

Needed Expense or Waste of Money?			
Description	Needed Expense	Waste of Money	Why
Oil change at dealership		X	Any repair shop or oil-change company can do the work for less. Make sure they use the correct oil for your car.

Major repairs at dealership		X	Find an independent repair shop to do the work. It will almost certainly be cheaper than the dealership.
Changing oil every 3,000 miles		X	Follow the schedule in the owner's manual for your particular car. Newer cars are now able to go at least 5,000 miles between oil changes.
Replacing belts and hoses whenever they are worn	X		Not repairing these small items immediately can cause your car to break down.
Following the maintenance schedule that the dealer recommends		X	The automaker knows your car best. Stick to the owner's manual.
Replacing the wipers at the repair shop		X	Replace the wipers so you can see, but do it yourself cheaply and easily.
Replacing the fuses or bulbs for the turn signals and brake lights at the repair shop		X	Buy fuses and bulbs on sale at the local auto store. Keep them in the glove compartment and fix them yourself.
Going to a top-rated ASE-certified (National Institute for Automotive Service Excellence) mechanic	X		A good mechanic is hard to find. If you find one, treat him gently and well.
Filling the gas tank with highest octane fuel		X	Check the owner's manual. A few high-performance cars need the higher grade, but most do fine on regular.

The Solutions

Car Maintenance You Can Still Do Yourself

Even with computers everywhere in cars today, there are still some maintenance tasks that you can do yourself. You save time and money by doing these tasks yourself and you know that the job will be done right.

Weekly

Check the coolant or antifreeze

This is an easy check because the radiator is at the front of the engine. If you have any doubts about where something is on your car, check the owner's manual. It should include a description with a diagram of what is under your hood.

Check Windshield Washer Fluid

This is usually a clear plastic reservoir up in front. You can buy the type of fluid recommended in your owner's manual at any auto parts store. When you top off the fluid, use a little of it on a rag to clean your windshield wiper blades.

Clean and Check Brake Lights, Turn Signals and Emergency Flashers

Buy spare light bulbs and fuses for these items at the auto parts store. Keep them in your glove compartment, so you can replace them at a moment's notice.

Do One Small Cleaning Task on the Car

Cleaning the car will be an easy task if you break it down into small, easy segments. For example, 1 week clean out the debris in your back seat. The next week, vacuum all the carpets. The week after that, clean all the windows inside and out, and so on.

Bi-Weekly

Check Air Conditioner in the Winter

If you live in a climate with cold winters, you need to remember to maintain your air conditioner even in winter. Keep all the parts lubricated by running the system for a few minutes.

Monthly

Check Belts and Hoses

Look under the hood at all the belts and hoses. Do any of the belts look frayed or worn? Replace them at the first sign of a problem. Hoses are ready for replacement when they feel hard or look worn.

Check Transmission Fluid

To check this component, your car needs to be running. Make sure to set the emergency brake. Shift the car from park to drive and back again. Remove the stick from the fluid and wipe it on a rag. Put it back into the fluid and take it out again. Look at it. There should be level markers along the stick. If your fluid is low, add the exact type recommended in your owner's manual. Be careful not to overfill the reservoir.

Check Oil Level

As with the transmission fluid, remove the stick and wipe it dry. Put it back in the reservoir and take it out again. Check the level marker. If the oil is low, add the type indicated in your owner's manual.

Inspect Brake Fluid

Read your manual to see exactly where the reservoir is for your car. You will probably have to pull off a clip or unscrew a lid. Check the fluid level markers, and add if needed. While you are putting the clip or lid back, take a minute to wipe it off.

Inspect Power Steering Fluid

Find the stick and check the levels. Add fluid if needed.

Check Tire Pressure and Tread Wear

You need to check the tire pressure when your car has been at rest for at least 3 hours. Use a pressure gauge to check the inflation level. If you need to drive to a gas station to get air, remember that warm tires cause a higher inflation reading. Do not overinflate.

Bi-Monthly

Inspect the Air Filter

You can check the air filter yourself or have it changed every time you get an oil change. Look at your owner's manual to see where it is on your particular engine. You need to replace it when it looks dirty.

Twice a Year

Check Shock Absorbers

This is an easy no-brainer check. Push the car up and down in a bouncing motion. Then step back. The car should not bounce again after you step away. If it does, you probably need to replace your shocks. Remember to replace two shocks at a time.

The Resources

The following Websites offer more information about how to maintain your automobile yourself:

www.nsc.org

The National Safety Council is a not-for-profit, non-governmental agency that advocates safe operation of all equipment.

www.cars.com

This Website includes information about maintenance on used and new cars.

www.energy.gov

This Website from the U.S. Department of Energy offers maintenance tips that will keep your car in good shape and increase your gas mileage.

What Can I Fix Myself?

Taking your car in for scheduled maintenance or repairs can be a humbling experience. If you know little or nothing about cars, you do not know if you should believe what the mechanic tells you or not. You face a huge dilemma when you go in for a scheduled oil change and find that the service manager recommends $500 in additional repairs for your new vehicle. This chapter will guide you through some basic repair terminology to make you feel more comfortable when you have to bring in your vehicle.

The Challenge

Today's vehicles are complicated pieces of machinery. The best basic information is a repair manual and a fast Internet connection. Repair manuals can be purchased either at an auto parts stores or at any general bookseller such as Barnes & Noble or Borders. These books explain all the working parts of your car and everything you need to understand how the engine works. The technicians themselves use a similar guide if they need to check a particular system on your car.

The Facts

Finding the Right Mechanic

It is important to find a mechanic before you actually need one, but finding the right mechanic or repair shop does not have to be difficult if you follow the tips below:

- Ask your circle of friends, relatives and co-workers for suggestions. If they like the shop and have taken their cars there for years, you know you have a potential candidate.
- Location is also important to consider when you are looking for a mechanic. If your brother-in-law just loves his mechanic, but it is located 15 miles from your home, this is not a good choice for you. The mechanic you choose should be conveniently located near your home or office.

- Call the shop to make sure that they work on your type of vehicle and will honor the warranty from the automaker. Ask about written estimates.
- Some warranties and service contracts require that you take your car to the dealership where you bought the car. Check the exact language to make sure that you can have another mechanic or shop do the repair and maintenance on your car.
- Visit the shop to see if you feel comfortable; ask how their work is priced and check if they have any accreditations such as ASE (Automotive Service Excellence). Ask which technicians are certified.
- Check with the shop about if they return used parts to the owner, how they charge for labor and if they charge for diagnostic services for your car. Are they able to hook cars up to a computerized machine to detect what is wrong with a car? If so, what do they charge for this service? Ask how they price their labor time. Some shops charge a flat fee for labor, and others charge exactly how many hours it took for a technician to do the repair.
- Call or go online to check with the Better Business Bureau.

The Solutions

Five Steps to Painless Auto Repair

1. Call your mechanic to make an appointment. Do not just stop by unless it is an emergency.

2. When you drop off the car, explain that you want a written estimate of the repairs or maintenance needed. They can usually e-mail or fax it to you. Make sure that you alert the service representative that you want a written estimate and do not want them to do any work until they get your permission.

Anatomy of a Written Estimate	
Condition to be repaired	This should include a description of the problem with the car.
Parts needed for repair	The description should include what type of parts will be used: new, remanufactured (also called rebuilt or reconditioned) or salvage. Your warranty can be invalidated if you use bad parts. Check the language before you agree to repairs with anything other than new parts.
Anticipated charge for labor	There may be some variance in this number because the service department may not know exactly how long the job will take. However, they should have done enough of this type of repair to be off only about 10 percent to 15 percent.
Signature of the service manager or technician	You want a signed estimate so that you know who to talk to about approval for the work. This is also the person to contact if you have questions about the repair.

Approval required before repairs will be attempted	Some states require that the car-owner approve car repairs. Even if your state does not have this rule, you can still stipulate to the shop that you want to approve the work AFTER you get the written estimate.

3. Look at their estimate. Call to ask for clarification or explanations. Then give your permission to do the work. If the price or explanations seem off to you, call another shop to ask for a second opinion.

4. When you pick up the car, ask the service manager or technician to go on a test drive with you to make sure that the problem has been fixed. While this step may seem a little excessive in your fast-paced life, you want to make sure that the shop knows that you will take them and their work on your car seriously. You do not want to have to come back again to get the same squeak fixed, so take the test drive first.

5. Go over the repair bill carefully. Ask the service manager or technician to explain any charge that you do not understand. The repair bill should include every action that the technician took along with the price of the part and the amount of labor required to put the part in place. Make sure you understand how the bill was prepared or calculated before you leave the shop.

6. Keep a record of all your repairs and maintenance. You will need this information if you ever have a problem with the shop or need to verify a date or specific repair. This information will also be very helpful if you decide to sell your car as it will provide written proof of your car's upkeep and history.

Other problems that can affect your car include recalls and technical service bulletins (TSBs). A recall occurs when the automaker alerts the media, car-owners and the government that there is a specific problem with a certain make, model and year of their car. In most cases, the manufacturer will send out a letter to everyone who bought that particular model and offer a free repair for the problem. You can check the automaker's Website to see if any recalls have been issued for your vehicle. In almost all cases, the automaker pays for the repairs on a recall.

Technical Service Bulletins (TSBs) are also used by automakers to alert consumers if a certain make, model or year of their car has had a number of complaints. The manufacturer is not necessarily admitting that there is a problem, but the TSB is sent to the service department of every dealership that sells that car. Searching for a TSB on your car is a good way to see if others are having the same problem that you are. You can also check if your car has any serious problems by going to the National Highway Traffic Safety Administration (NHTSA) Website to scope things out.

The Resources

The following Websites offer more information about how to understand car repair:

www.aaa.com

The American Automobile Association's (also called AAA or Triple A) Website has a variety of information about finding good mechanics and how to deal with breakdowns on the highway.

www.ftc.gov

The Federal Trade Commission's (FTC) Website contains useful information about auto repairs and other car-related matters.

www.naag.org

The National Association of Attorneys General offers a Website with a variety of information for consumers including information about what to do if you suspect your mechanic is overcharging or misleading you.

www.bbb.org

Check out the Better Business Bureau's (BBB) Website when you are considering possible mechanics. This should be done before you visit any potential shop. The site will alert you to any serious complaints that have been lodged against the shop and prevent you from wasting valuable time and money.

www-odi.nhtsa.dot.gov/cars/problems/recalls/recallsearch.cfm

This Website from the NHTSA includes a database to search for any recall or technical service bulletins about your car.

How Can I Improve Gas Mileage?

Whether you are buying a new car or driving an old one, you are undoubtedly interested in getting better gas mileage. Some people use gas additives or other devices that claim to improve gas mileage even on old cars. Other people keep their driving habits in check to save money at the gas pump. While gas additives and fuel tank magnets do not work, improving your own driving can save you both gas and money.

The Challenge

New cars have an estimated mileage rating on the sticker. However, the estimated mileage per gallon may be off by 10 to 20 percent. As you know you can save gas and get better mileage just by watching how you drive in addition to being aware of your destinations. The driver has the greatest effect on gas mileage–even more than a new fuel-efficient vehicle.

The Facts

All about Octane

You can get the best mileage on your car by using the gasoline recommended in your owner's manual. For most cars that means regular fuel. A few specific cars, primarily sports cars, luxury vehicles, and SUVs (sport utility vehicles) require a higher octane.

Octane ratings show a gasoline's ability to resist engine knock. Engine knock is a pinging or rattle that is caused by premature ignition of fuel and air in one or more cylinders of your car. Octane is indicated on yellow stickers on the gas pumps. Regular gas typically has an octane rating of 87 while mid-grade gasoline usually has an octane rating of 89. Premium-grade gasoline is usually 92 or 93 octane. Not surprisingly, octane ratings differ across the country. Each state has different octane requirements for each grade of gasoline.

Using a higher octane than is recommended in your owner's manual will not improve your mileage nor will it make your car perform better, go faster or run cleaner, according to the Federal Trade Commission (FTC). Do not be fooled by advertisements; follow the recommendations in your owner's manual.

AFVs or Hybrid Cars

The U.S. Department of Energy suggests that those who really want to save money on gas and achieve excellent gas mileage should consider using alternative fuel vehicles (AFVs) or hybrid cars. AFVs operate on fuels such as ethanol, methanol, electricity and compressed natural gas. These fuels can reduce the harmful pollutants in the air and exhaust emissions.

According to the DOE, hybrid electric vehicles (HEVs) combine the best of gasoline engines with electric motors to achieve excellent gas mileage and fuel efficiency. They also emit fewer exhaust fumes and pollutants.

The Solutions

Regular Maintenance

One key to excellent gas mileage is to carefully maintain your vehicle according to the standards set out in your owner's manual. Follow the tips below to save yourself money on gasoline:

Tune Engine

Depending on the condition and age of your car, you can increase your average mileage approximately 4 percent just by keeping your engine tuned up. Pay attention to the requirements listed in your owner's manual and take your car in for service as the manual suggests.

Inflate Tires Properly and Align Wheels

According to the FTC, you can add about 3 percent to your mileage just by making sure that your tires are inflated properly and aligned. The proper inflation is listed in your owner's manual. You will need to get your tires aligned whenever you buy new tires, have a flat or go over especially rough terrain. If you normally drive only in the city, you will not need to get your wheels aligned very often.

Change Oil

You can also save gas by changing your oil as often as the owner's manual suggests. Older cars typically need to have the oil changed every 5,000 to 7,000 miles. These days, many manufacturers suggest changing the oil on new cars every 3,000 miles.

According to the Department of Energy (DOE) and the Environmental Protection Agency (EPA), you can improve mileage by using the grade of motor oil that is recommended in your owner's manual. Oil that advertises itself as energy conserving and includes the logo of the American Petroleum Institute can improve fuel efficiency by using friction-reducing additives.

Replace Air Filters

You can improve your mileage by about 10 percent if you routinely replace clogged air filters when you get your oil changed.

Efficient Driving

Besides keeping your car in good repair, the other key to getting good gas mileage is careful and efficient driving. Follow the tips below to improve your vehicle's fuel efficiency and mileage:

Drive Gently

Experts advise that cars get better gas mileage and fuel economy on the highway. But if you spend most of your time driving in the city, you can get better mileage by avoiding jackrabbit starts and stops in city traffic. Anticipate the ebb and flow of traffic and drive gently. Racing to a red light burns fuel. If you approach the intersection slowly when the light is red, you may find the light has changed to green before you have to brake. This also saves gasoline.

Stay within Speed Limit

Driving at speeds over 60 miles per hour decreases gas mileage and efficiency. To improve your efficiency, stick with the posted speed limit at all times.

Do Not Pack Top of Car

You can lose up to 5 percent of your fuel economy by loading your vacation supplies on the roof of your car or in a roof carrier. The wind resistance causes you to use more fuel. If you can pack more carefully and fit everything within your car, you will save gasoline.

Remove Extra Weight from Trunk

If you live in a climate with frosty winters, you may put bags of sand or kitty litter in your trunk during the coldest months. However, that extra weight is stealing fuel efficiency. In the warmer months, lighten up your trunk for an average of 5 percent better mileage and fuel efficiency.

When Necessary, Use Overdrive or Cruise Control

If you have a vehicle with overdrive or cruise control, use these features when you are driving on the highway. According to the FTC and the DOE, these features save gas and provide better mileage than if you were controlling the car all on your own.

Combine Errands

Restarting your engine several times for short trips uses twice as much energy as driving when the engine is warm. For this reason, try to combine short trips together and do them all at once. You will save gas, improve your car's mileage and reduce pollution.

Stop Idling

Keeping your car running at idle wastes gasoline and pollutes the atmosphere. If you need to wait for more than a minute or two, turn the engine off. You will be saving yourself money.

Use Public Transportation When Possible

If you live in an urban area, consider taking public transportation to most of your destinations. You will help yourself by providing exercise, limiting pollution and saving money on gasoline. If biking to work or walking is an option, consider improving your own health while you save energy.

Carpool to Work

Some cities have online services to match up commuters who drive from the same general area. If you drive to work alone most days, you can save money, gas and pollution by finding a carpool group. Some cities even have special faster lanes for those who carpool with three or more people.

The Resources

The following Websites offer more information about how to get better mileage no matter what kind of car you drive:

www.ftc.gov

The FTC Website has wonderful information. In addition, you can download many helpful PDF documents. Two of the best are: *Good, Better, Best: How to Improve Gas Mileage* and *Saving Starts @ Home: The Inside Story on Conserving Energy*.

www.fueleconomy.gov

This Website from the Department of Energy contains information about alternative fuel and hybrid vehicles.

www.afdc.doe.gov

The Department of Energy's Alternative Fuels Data Center Website is filled with great information on all aspects of alternative fuels and saving energy.

What If My Car Is Stolen or Breaks Down?

Most car consumers conduct research to find the safest cars on the market and buy the latest safety devices for their family. However, few consumers know how to avoid safety concerns such as carjacking, car theft or injuries during a car breakdown.

The Challenge

You hope that it never happens to you, but carjacking, car theft and car breakdowns occur every day. Do you know what to do to protect yourself and your family? You can avoid potential carjacking, car theft situations and follow proper safety precautions in the event that your car breaks down with the right information. Being prepared and knowing what to do can ease your mind during stressful and potentially dangerous events.

The Facts

Car Breakdown Tips for Safety

Do you know how to save your life if your car breaks down on the highway or in the city? The most important safety tip is the most obvious: stay out of traffic.

Avoiding Injuries When Your Car Breaks Down	
To Avoid Problems	**Correct Action To Take**
On the highway, stay in the car after a breakdown.	Drive the car to a safe place where you can examine the damage. You need plenty of room away from traffic to look at your car. Do not try to park by the side of a busy road and check the damage. Passing cars could hit you or your car accidentally.
If you cannot move the vehicle, stay inside with doors and windows locked. Turn on the flashers.	Use your cell phone to call for help. Do not stand outside the vehicle. A passing car can hit you or criminals could pretend they are stopping to help you.

Do not try to repair your car or tire on the shoulder of the road.	Drive the car to a safe place before you attempt to change the tire. Ruin your wheel, rim or tire, but do not fix a flat too close to a highway.
Carry appropriate emergency materials in your trunk.	In addition to the usual tire-changing materials, carry a few more emergency items to help you if you have a breakdown. Carry a can of emergency tire inflator. A stand-alone battery charger will enable you to restart your car by yourself. In addition, carry flares or emergency cones to indicate your car's position on the roadway. If it is safe to get out and place them, do so.

The Solutions

Preventing Carjacking

You can protect yourself from most carjacking incidents if you keep alert and follow the tips below.

Avoiding Carjacking and Minimizing the Damage	
To Avoid Problems	**What Could Happen**
Never leave your car running.	Do not just run into the store for a minute and leave your car running. Never leave your children alone.
Do not park in dark or isolated areas, use cash machines or pay phones in these areas.	Carjackers lurk in dark places with few people passing by. Some carjacking incidents are spur of the moment. A person may see you in a dangerous location and decide to carjack you.
Whether you are in the car or outside of it, keep the windows up and the doors locked.	Carjacking can take place in parking lots. Keep the doors and windows locked even when you are in your car eating lunch or making a call on your cell phone.
Stay alert and look around you.	Be careful as you walk from a store to your car in the parking lot. Be watchful of anyone standing around. Even those near another car could be carjackers.
Be alert to people at bus stops or hanging around outside a gas station.	Some carjackers specialize in stealing cars when the owners stop for gasoline. As you are filling up your vehicle, keep alert for people milling around.
Dangerous situations	
If another car hits you, do not stop and get out. Keep the doors locked and the windows up.	One common carjacking trick is to run into your car and then ask you to stop to trade-insurance information. Do not stop. Call the police on your cell phone or drive to the closest police station.

If someone approaches you or your vehicle, think only of your own life and that of any passengers or children.	If someone tries to carjack you, give him or her the car and protect yourself and your family first. Once you and your family are safe, then you can worry about what you left inside the car, inside a purse or inside a briefcase or backpack.

Preventing Auto Theft

You can prevent auto theft by following good safety precautions every time that you get into or out of your vehicle. Follow the tips below:

Tips to Protect Yourself From Auto Theft	
Theft Prevention Step	**Results and Explanation**
If possible, park your car in a locked garage.	Your car will be twice as safe if it is locked in a locked garage. Car thieves do not want to spend too much time stealing. Make it as difficult for them as you can.
Leave packages, backpacks, briefcase and any other valuable items in the trunk.	Do not cover these items with a blanket or park under a streetlight. Thieves often find targets of opportunity. If they think you have something valuable in the backseat, they may decide to break in or steal the whole car.
Use a lock on your steering wheel. You can also use a lock on the column of your gearshift.	Locking the steering wheel or the gearshift makes it impossible for thieves to drive away with your car. They will look for vehicles without these items because those cars are easier to steal.
Lock your car even in the garage. Lock it when you park it on the street or in a parking lot.	Lock your car as well as using a security system if one has been installed on your car. Make it as difficult as possible for thieves.
Keep your vehicle registration safe in your wallet. Do not keep it in the glove box.	If your car is stolen, you will not have to worry about identity theft if you have your vehicle registration information in your wallet.
Use etching, paint or an indelible market to put your VIN number on various components of your car.	Car thieves often steal cars so that the vehicle can be sold for parts. If you write the Vehicle Identification Number (VIN) on the car's battery, under the hood, on the engine and under the hood of the trunk, you will make it more difficult for thieves to disguise the various parts of your car.

Be Prepared

You hope it never happens, but you can make your life much easier if you have the right information available if your car is stolen. Your first action should be to call the police.

Use the chart on the following page to prepare for the proper information to give to the authorities:

Be Prepared With the Correct Information for Police	
Make sure you know the color, make, model, year and VIN of your car.	In addition to this basic information, make sure that you can describe any additional after-market items on your car such as a sunroof, moon roof, special wheels or a new stereo or CD player.
Know when you found the car gone and approximately when you think it was stolen.	Try to recreate the last time that you saw the car or when you last drove it.
Have descriptions of anyone lurking near your car or in the neighborhood just before your car was stolen.	Car thieves often walk neighborhoods looking for likely targets. Think back to anyone hanging around the neighborhood or anyone you do not recognize as a neighbor.
The name, address and telephone number of anyone who may have witnessed the car being stolen.	If possible, give the police a list of people or neighbors who might have seen or heard something when your car was stolen. Any information you can give the police will make their job easier.

The Resources

The following Websites offer more tips about protecting yourself from car theft, carjacking and accidents during a breakdown:

www.cityofmesa.org/police/literature/pdf/veh_security.pdf

The city of Mesa, Arizona offers a flyer with information about protecting yourself and your car from thieves.

www.nctcog.org/cs/ratt/pdf/carjack.pdf

Download this brochure about carjacking from the North Central Texas Council of Governments and the Texas Department of Transportation.

www.ci.el-paso.tx.us/police/prevent.asp

The City of El Paso, Texas has a list of 50 ways to prevent car theft.

www.s2w.org

This Website, Safe Smart Women, is sponsored by the CarMax Foundation and offers a variety of articles and tips to help women to be safe on the road.

How Do I Compare Cars & Deals?

When you begin researching your new or used car purchase or your lease, you need a way to keep track of all the various prices, options and possibilities inherent in the process. This chapter provides complete versions of checklists for the new car buyer, the used car buyer and one for those looking to lease a vehicle. These comprehensive checklists should provide you with an excellent way to manage all the information you find on your journey to obtain the perfect vehicle.

The Challenge

Use these checklists when you are researching your car options before you visit the dealership. You can also use this information to help you make a better deal at the dealership, with a private owner and with the F&I manager.

The Facts

Used Car Buying Checklist

Use this checklist if you are buying a used car from a private owner. Use the new car checklist if you are buying a car from the dealership.

Comparing Used Cars from Private Owners			
General Information	**Car 1**	**Car 2**	**Car 3**
Make and model of car			
Seats how many passengers?			
Amount of truck space?			
Amount of cargo space?			
Mileage of car?			
Age of car?			
Miscellaneous option			
Miscellaneous option			

Miscellaneous option			
Maintenance records for car			
Proof of oil changes, etc.			
Price: Total asking price of car:			
Minus (-)			
Costs to repair			
Mechanic recommendations to fix:			
A.			
B.			
C.			
Cost for new paint?			
Cost for new tires?			
Cost to fix rust spots?			
Insurance costs			
Gas costs			
Parking costs			
Equals (=)			
True cost to own car:			

Leasing Checklist

You can download a complete *Federal Consumer Leasing Act Disclosure* form from the FTC at *www.ftc.com*. However, you should start by using the new car checklist to figure out how much room you have to negotiate with the dealer.

Truth in Leasing Information			
General Information	**Car 1**	**Car 2**	**Car 3**
Make and model of car			
Amount due at lease signing or delivery			
Capitalized cost reduction			
First monthly payment			
Refundable security deposit			
Title fees			
Registration fees			
Miscellaneous fees			
Total			

Gross capitalized cost (agreed upon value of vehicle)			
Capitalized cost reduction (trade-in or down payment)			
Adjusted capitalized cost (used to calculate your base monthly payment)			
Residual value (value of vehicle at end of lease period)			
Rent charge			
Total of the monthly payments including the depreciation and any amortized amounts plus the rent charge			
Lease payments (the number of payments in your lease)			
Base monthly payment			
Monthly sales/use tax			
Total monthly payment			

The Solutions

The New Car Buyer's Checklist

If you are thinking about buying a new car, this checklist will help you decide on the perfect vehicle and options for your purchase. Fill one out for every car you car considering and you should be able to compare vehicles in an apples-to-apples fashion.

New Car Checklist*			
	Car 1	**Invoice Price**	**Sticker Price**
Make and model of car:			
OPTIONS			
Transmission: Auto or manual?			
Air-conditioning			
Engine size			
Audio system with am/fm			
Audio with CD player			
Audio with CD changer			
Brakes: Antilock or power assist			
Power locks			
Power windows			
Seats: Power			

	Car 1	Invoice Price	Sticker Price
Seats: heated			
Seats: Leather			
Rear window: Wiper			
Rear window: Defroster			
Wheels and tires			
Alloy wheels			
All season tires			
Mirrors and lights			
Map lights			
Illuminated dual vanity lights			
Exterior power mirrors			
Heated mirrors			
Safety options			
LATCH			
Side-impact airbags			
Curtain-type airbags			
Alarm system			
Built-in cell phone/Hands-Free Device			
Remote keyless entry			
Sunroof or moon roof			
Miscellaneous option			
Miscellaneous option			
Miscellaneous option			
Miscellaneous option			
Totals:			

*Information provided by the FTH

50

What Other Resources Are Available?

You can find incredible amounts of information when it comes to buying a car by looking on the Internet. In addition to general information, there are online calculators, comparisons charts and checklist designed to help you, the consumer, arm yourself with the best knowledge to help you get the best deal. Here is a complete list of Websites to help you buy a new or used car, lease a car and negotiate every part of the process. Some Websites are specifically targeted to one aspect of your car transaction, where other Websites are so complete that they have information on almost every aspect of car buying and leasing.

Car Auctions

www.treas.gov/auctions/customs
www.autoauctions.gsa.gov
*http://gsaauctions.gov/gsauctions/
gsaauctions*
*www.usdoj.gov/marshals/assets/
nsl.html*
www.pueblo.gsa.gov
*www.leaseguide.com/articles/
carauctions.htm*

Buying a New Car

www.cars.com
www.nadaguides.com
www.autodealer.com
www.ftc.gov
www.edmunds.com

Buying a Used Car

www.carfax.com
www.cars.com
www.nadaguides.com

www.ftc.gov
www.autodealer.com
www.edmunds.com
*www.safecarguide.com/gui/new/
usedcars.htm*
*www.beatthecarsalesman.com/
mailbag18.html*
*www.is-it-a-lemon.com/vehicle_
history/faq-fleet.htm*

Car Jacking

*www.cityofmesa.org/police/
literature/pdf/veh_security.pdf*
*www.nctcog.org/cs/ratt/pdf/
carjack.pdf*
*www.ci.el-paso.tx.us/police/
prevent.asp*
www.s2w.org/

Car-Sharing

www.flexcar.com
www.igocars.org
www.cnt.org

Choosing a Car

*www.partsamerica.com/
maintenanceailingcar.aspx*
www.kbb.com
*www.doityourself.com/stry/
distancetips*
www.cars.com
www.nadaguides.com
www.edmunds.com
www.geico.com
www.esurance.com
www.insureone.com
www.carfax.com

Donating a Car

*www.bbb.org/alerts/article.
asp?ID=498*
www.give.org
www/irs.gov
*www.cartalk.com/content/features/
vehicledonation/#howitworks*
*www.donatecarusa.com/index.
php?promo=NADA*

Financing

www.ftc.gov
www.aaa.com
www.autofinancing101.org
www.bbb.org
www.simpleliving.net
www.equifax.com
www.experian.com
www.transunion.com
www.making-change.org
www.autofinancing101.org
www.bbb.org
www.naag.org

Hybrid Cars

www.fueleconomy.gov
www.eere.energy.gov/cleancities
www.safercar.gov
www.hybridcars.com
*www.msnbc.msn.com/
id/12958916/site/newsweek*

Insurance

www.naag.org
*www.ftc.gov/ftc/consumer/home.
html*
www.naic.org/
www.nhtsa.gov/
www.consumerfed.org
www.aaa.com
*https://www.nicb.org/cps/rde/xchg/
SID-4031FE95-C7D6B80/nicb/
hs.xsl/75.htm*
www.iii.org/individuals/auto
*www.bbb.org/alerts/article.
asp?ID=431*

Leasing

www.leasesource.com
www.swapalease.com
www.cars.com
www.autotrader.com
www.nadaguide.com
www.edmunds.com
*www.pueblo.gsa.gov/cic_text/cars/
key2leas/default.htm*
www.ftc.gov/autos
www.nvla.org

Lemon Laws

*www.nationallemonlawcenter.
com/lemon-law-tips.htm*
*www.autopedia.com/html/
HotLinks_Lemon2.html*
*www.autopedia.com/html/MfgSites.
html*
www.lemonlaw.bbb.org/
www.carfax.com
*www.alldata.com/recalls/index.
html*

Maintenance

www.cars.com
*www1.eere.energy.gov/consumer/
tips/driving.html*
www.fueleconomy.gov/
www.afdc.doe.gov
www.aaa.com
www.naag.org/
www.bbb.org
*www-odi.nhtsa.dot.gov/cars/
problems/recalls/recallsearch.cfm*

Negotiating

*http://about.edmunds.com/advice/
buying/articles/42962/page001.
html*
www.aaa.com
www.ftc.gov
www.naag.org

No Haggle/
No Hassle Car Buying

www.aaa.com
www.edmunds.com
www.cars.com
www.invoicedealers.com
www.carsdirect.com
www.acscorp.com
*www.costcoauto.com/howworks/
faqs.asp*
*www.addisonavenue.com/content/
shared/articles/buy_rental.asp*

Ordering a New Car

*www.carbuyingtips.com/carintro.
html*
*http://beatthecarsalesman.com/
mailbag21.html*
www.naag.org
www.nada.org

Renting a Car

*www.ag.state.mn.us/consumer/
cars/CarHandbook/CarHnbk_
4.htm*
www.ftc.gov
*www.bbb.org/alerts/article.
asp?ID=96*

Rebates and Incentives

*http://blogs.cars.com/kickingtires/
incentives/*
*www.cars.com/go/advice/
incentives/incentivesAll.jsp*
*www.cars.com/go/advice/
financing/calc/incentivesCalc.jsp*
*www.nadaguides.com/home.
aspx?l=1&w=28&p=0&f=5000*

Resale Value

www.cars.com
www.nadaguides.com
www.ftc.gov
www.aaa.com
www.iii.org
www.kbb.com

Researching Cars

www.kbb.com
www.autodealer.com
www.cars.com
www.nadaguides.com
www.ftc.gov
www.edmunds.com

Safety

www.kbb.com
*www.insidercarsecrets.com
defensive_driving.html*
www.nsc.org
www.nhtsa.dot.org
*www.tiresafety.com/images/
Mario_brochure.pdf*
www.tiresafety.com
www.rma.org/tire_safety
*www.michelinman.com/mastapp/
servlet/Controller/site.care.
MainPage*
www.safercar.gov
www.hwysafety.org
www.iii.org

Scams

www.bbb.org
*www.ftc.gov/ftc/consumer/home.
html*
www.naag.org/
*www.fbi.gov/cyberinvest/
cyberhome.htm*
*www.usdoj.gov/criminal/
cybercrime/reporting.htm*
www.nicb.org

Technology

*www.intellichoice.com/
carBuying101/Telematics*

Teen Car/First Car

www.iihs.org/ratings/default.aspx
www.iii.org
www.nhtsa.dot.gov/ncap/Index.cfm
www.consumerfed.org
www.aaa.com
www.nicb.org
www.nsc.org
www.cars.com
www.autotrader.com
*www1.eere.energy.gov/consumer/
tips/driving.html*

Test Drive

*www.mynrma.com.au/easy_
guides_taking_test_drive.asp*
www.autotrader.com
www.kbb.com
*www.automotive.com/Buy_New/
Car_Buying_Tips/car-test-drives.
aspx*
www.carsearch.com/buy-new.html
www.carmarket.com/testdrive.cfm

Trade-in

www.autotrader.com
www.nadaguides.com
www.edmunds.com
www.carfax.com

Index

Smart, Friendly and Informative

The *50 plus one* series are thorough and detailed guides covering a wide range of topics–both personal and business related, supplying you, the reader, the information and resources you need and want in an easy-to-read format.

50 plus one Tips When Remodeling Your Home
by William Resch

50 plus one Tips to Building a Retirement Nest Egg
by Linda M. Magoon and Poonum Vasishth

50 plus one Tips When Hiring & Firing Employees
Edited by Linda M. Magoon & Donna de St. Aubin

50 plus one Tips to Preventing Identity Theft
by Elizabeth Drake

50 plus one Questions to Ask Your Doctor
by Elizabeth Drake

50 plus one Greatest Sports Heroes of All Times
(North American edition)
by Paul J. Christopher

50 plus one Ways to Improve Your Study Habits
by Stephen Edwards

50 plus one Great Books You Should Have Read
(and probably didn't)
by George Walsh

50 plus one Greatest Cities In the World You Should Visit
by Paul J. Christopher

Titles from Encouragement Press

Available from bookstores everywhere or directly from Encouragement Press. Bulk discounts are available, for information please call 1.253.303.0033

50 plus one Series			
Title	Price	Qty.	Subtotal
Greatest Cities in the World You Should Visit	$14.95 U.S./$19.95 Can.		
Tips When Remodeling Your Home	$14.95 U.S./$19.95 Can.		
Greatest Sports Heroes of All Times (North American edition)	$14.95 U.S./$19.95 Can.		
Tips to Building A Retirement Nest Egg	$14.95 U.S./$19.95 Can.		
Ways To Improve Your Study Habits	$14.95 U.S./$19.95 Can.		
Tips When Hiring & Firing Employees	$14.95 U.S./$19.95 Can.		
Questions When Buying a Car	$14.95 U.S./$19.95 Can.		
Tips to Preventing Identity Theft	$14.95 U.S./$19.95 Can.		
Great Books You Should Have Read (and probably didn't)	$14.95 U.S./$19.95 Can.		
Questions to Ask Your Doctor	$14.95 U.S./$19.95 Can.		
		Subtotal	
		IL residents add 8.75% sales tax	
		Shipping & Handling*	
		Total	

* Shipping & Handling

U.S. Orders:	Canadian Orders:
$3.35 for first book	$7.00 for first book
$2.00 for ea. add'l add book	$5.00 for ea. add'l book

4 Ways to Order

Phone: 1.773.262.6565

Web: *www.encouragementpress.com*

Fax: 1.773.262.9765

**Mail: Encouragement Press LLC
1261 W. Glenlake
Chicago, IL 60660**

Please make checks payable to:
Encouragement Press, LLC
*(Orders must be prepaid. We regret that
we are unable to ship orders without
payment or purchase order)*

Payment Method (check one)
❏ Check enclosed ❏ Visa ❏ MasterCard

_____
card number

_____
signature

_____
Name as it appears on card

expiration date _____

P.O. #_____

Encouragement Press, LLC
1261 W. Glenlake • Chicago, IL 60660 • *sales@encouragementpress.com*